NOELLE MOORE

MORE THAN

I'M SORRY

I0379360

How To Help Any Mom
After the Loss of their Child
Using a Proven Step-by-Step Model

Copyright © 2022 Noelle Moore

All rights reserved.

No part of this book may be reproduced, scanned, or distributed in any printed or electronic form without express written permission from the author.

ISBN 978-1-939237-92-7

Published by Suncoast Digital Press, Inc.
Sarasota, Florida, U.S.A.

Credits: The Finley Project®

With permission and appreciation,
the graphics and materials of the model
which are included in this book
are original to The Finley Project®

https://www.thefinleyproject.org

CONTENTS

Dedication v
Foreword vii
The Sunshine Years 1
Painting a Beautiful Future 13
No Words. 17
My Daughter 27
My Husband 45
The Outsider 53
A Map of Hope for the Lost 65
My Daughter's Forever Legacy: The Finley Project® 77
The Finley Project 7-Part Holistic Model and Program 83
The Finley Project Model® 87
(1) AID 93
(2) NOURISH 97
(3) CLEANSE 101
(4) RESTORE 107
(5) FELLOWSHIP 111
(6) COUNSEL 117
(7) SUPPORT 123
Honor and Hope 129
My Mission to Improve Mother's Care in Hospitals 137
Afterword 143
Resources and Consulting 149
Gift Ideas For Moms 151
Contact Us 155

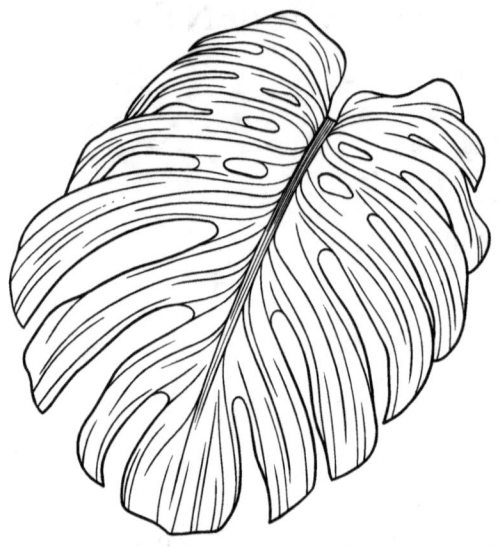

Leaves are timeless symbols of life, growth, protection, and renewal. In sacred text, they represent both fragility and durability; both hope and hardships.

Through leaves, we receive oxygen. Let each leaf in this book give you energy and hope, just as you bring those to others. Let each chapter help you help someone else turn over a new leaf.

DEDICATION

For moms healing a broken heart — I dedicate this book to you, so that you may know you are never, ever alone, never forgotten, and never overlooked. You are forever your son's or daughter's mommy.

To my mother and father, "Pops" — I love you and am so thankful to call you my parents. You are the reason for this book. Your strength, your character and love for God, inspires me through today.

Rest in Peace

John Carroll "Pops" Moore	Finley Elizabeth Oblander
Sempre Fie	Psalm 139
February 13, 2013	August 16, 2013

FOREWORD

By Anthony J. Orsini, D.O.
Board Certified Neonatologist

A more devastating and tragic life-event than experiencing the death of a newborn baby is impossible to imagine. As a neonatologist for over 25 years, I have seen far too many mothers and fathers hold their baby as they say goodbye. Sadly, many do not even get that chance as the loss hits suddenly, ending their hopes and dreams quickly. In a moment's time, parents and their lives are redefined. The group they become part of, the other parents who live with this kind of grief, is a club no one wants to join. This tragic loss of a child cannot be understood nor imagined by anyone who has not experienced it.

Even without full understanding, we recognize the parents' pain. During this life-changing event, compassionate healthcare professionals, family, and friends attempt to provide what little comfort and support they can. But what happens after a mother leaves the hospital without her baby? What happens when the doctors and nurses say goodbye with hugs and prayers? Or after family and friends go home, leaving a mother and father with nothing but a silent nursery, an empty crib, and tearful thoughts of what should have been?

Far too many mothers are left with nothing but distress and unanswered questions: *What do I do now? Where do I turn?* These answers can only be sufficiently provided by others who have experienced similar losses. Through the tragedy of losing her precious daughter Finley, Noelle Moore has risen from the deepest, darkest time of her life to finding a new purpose. Recognizing that society has not yet found a way to help mothers who have lost their babies, Noelle started The Finley Project to help parents when society has failed to do so. I have known Noelle Moore for over 10 years and I am honored to call her a friend and a colleague. I have seen firsthand the profound difference that she and her Foundation are making in the world.

In this book, as only a mother who has experienced it can, Noelle explains the emotions and impact of losing a child. She provides practical guidance to parents who have experienced loss and to their loved ones who want to help. As Noelle eloquently states, "The mom doesn't need you to feel the pain that they feel, they need you to help them get through it."

But how can we help someone "get through it?" What could be said or done that would be the right kind of support? For the first time, there's real help—there's a proven step-by-step system developed and utilized by Noelle and The Finley Project. Whether you are a parent who has experienced the loss of a child or someone who has struggled to help a friend or family member ease the pain, this is a must-read book. As a healthcare professional, I dream of the day when we can prevent all infant loss. Until then, reading Noelle's book is a major step toward helping those who need us the most.

Anthony J. Orsini, D.O.
Board Certified Neonatologist
Author, *It's All in the Delivery – Helping Families When They Need Us the Most*
CEO of The Orsini Way

THE FINLEY PROJECT MODEL

What Others are Saying

"During this period of intense grief, Moore realized that there were very few holistic resources aimed at helping mothers get through the most catastrophic stages of loss, and decided to start an organization of her own, which became The Finley Project."

—People Magazine (May 18, 2021). "After Losing Their Own Babies, These Women Now Help Others Get Through 'Literally, Your Worst Nightmare'."

"I was in a really bad place and I didn't want to live any more. I wasn't leaving my house and I was a shell of a person. You lose yourself, but The Finley Project came in and brought me back to life. The cleanings helped me feel human again, the massages released tension, and the Counseling made me feel like my grief was normal. The meet-ups made me feel like I was in a safe place."

—Maria Felton, a mother in The Finley Project Program, lost her 10-month-old son, MJ

"The Finley Project has found a way to turn tragedy into beauty. Their devotion to grieving mothers is incredibly heartwarming and we are honored to be a part of the healing process. The benefits of massage are numerous especially when the recipient is in a state of grief. Grief is a prime contributor to stress and stress can have long-term effects on the body. Massage can assist with the physical and even emotional ramifications associated with grief."

—Erika and Michel Sasser, Owners, Massage Envy Spa®, Altamonte Springs, Florida

"The Finley Project helped in so many ways. The house cleaners were a blessing because I was recovering from emergency surgery. My husband had lost his job right before our loss so the gift cards for food helped keep us fed. I'm still seeing the amazing counselor they found for me and more than anything, The Finley Project helped me not feel so alone in all of this."

—Danielle Koch, a mother in The Finley Project Program, lost her daughter, Kaylin, during labor

More Than "I'm Sorry"

CHAPTER 1

The Sunshine Years

…That night was horrific. I could hear the overheard speakers play a lullaby every time a baby was born. Every…single…time. I was in so much pain and felt so alone. I couldn't sleep. Around 4 a.m., I finally fell asleep, only to wake up to my alarm at 6 a.m. Flashes of images and blurry thoughts filled my mind. Was it a nightmare? Did all that really happen? I quickly realized it was not a terrifying dream, but real—and that I needed to get on that ambulance to find my newborn daughter…

My name is Noelle Moore and I survived the unimaginable.

My life, as I will share in the pages to follow, was solid, growing up. From having a faith-filled family to experiencing lovely adventures during my entire upbringing, I felt very blessed, to say the least. However, that all changed in 2013. My *normal* was no longer normal for me. I was forever changed.

As a child, I was smart. I was one of those kids that loved school, could learn fairly well, but worked hard at getting good grades. I wanted to be the best at everything. My young life was delightful, overall. Palm trees filled our front yard, along with bikes strewn in the grass. Summertime meant kids flipping cartwheels on the sidewalk and basketballs bouncing in the driveway. Inside our home, piano-playing filled hours of time; all-day delicious smells of crockpot meals were a usual thing, and a television with the latest news was almost always blaring.

I knew very little of hardship; indeed, our family chose to laugh a lot. The vitality and light-heartedness in our home was contagious. Friends would want to come to my house to play because it was fun. We laughed a lot in our family and so did they.

There were so many of us—eight, to be exact—a his-hers-and-ours family. My parents were "older" parents, my mother being 40 when she had me and my father being 48. I had one "real" brother (as I used to say), 17 months older. Patrick Christopher. We were super close. My mom was beautiful, kind, and funny. She worked at a local church preschool and was the best teacher I had ever seen. She knew how to command a room—even one full of rambunctious toddlers. My father was the dad of all dads. Sitting on the floor in front of him while he brushed and dried my hair, I felt his full attention and unconditional love surrounding me, a special bonding time I could count on every week. My father could walk into a room and have 10 best friends within 20 minutes; my dad loved people and they loved him.

Linnie & John Moore (1983)

One particular Thanksgiving when I was a skinny 7-year-old girl, I remember sitting down to our large solid oak "formal" table, set with blue-flowered napkins and crowded with turkey, dressing, baskets of rolls, bowls brimming over with salads, mashed potatoes, and cranberry sauce. Each member of our large family settled into a chair and my father said a Blessing. Then, breaking the stillness, my dad picked up a basket of rolls and pitched one to me to catch! Always joking around, he proceeded to toss one to each of us. That was my dad—funny, kind, entertaining, and always "Mr. Hospitality."

The Sunshine Years

I grew up dreaming of all things BIG. I never wanted to be ordinary or normal—and was actually never quite normal. I thought maybe acting was going to be in my future. Or maybe I'd be an attorney by day and an actress by night? Also, I did have a natural talent for sports, with one exception.

When I was nine, my parents signed me up for recreational soccer through the local Recreation Center. I was super excited. I went with my mother to the sports store to buy cleats, a ball, and shin guards. She warned me that I better "stick with it" because the gear "cost an arm and a leg." Lo and behold, I did not stick with it. At my very first practice, dressed in the expensive garb, I took a ball shot right at my ear and cried and cried. That's the first time I think I had ever cried like that. I begged my mom to leave and so we did. My mother was mildly sympathetic yet incredibly annoyed as I whined that I was never playing soccer again. My cleats, my ball, and my brand-new shin guards were placed on the garage shelving unit. Soccer was not my thing.

Moore Family, Franklin, NC (2012)

But then I went on into middle school to play basketball, volleyball, softball, and run track. I was, what most told me, a "natural athlete" and indeed I did receive collegiate volleyball scholarship offers. I eventually settled on a small, liberal arts school in my hometown in order to stay near family and friends. I adored the school, the beautiful lakeside campus, and the rich history. Some would call it a small "country club." I can imagine it as a setting for a movie about upper echelon college kids from the North attending a college in the South. The buildings and campus dripped with Southern charm as thick as the Spanish moss hanging from its sprawling oak trees.

I loved campus life and playing volleyball. I even wanted to join a sorority to meet more people and I did just that. I felt happy, excited, and accomplished. Playing volleyball was tough and felt like a full-time job—practices started at 5 a.m. some days and night games kept us up until midnight. It took a disciplined person to maintain schoolwork, friendships, and family life. I learned a lot during that time, mostly self-discipline, but also I developed some lifelong friendships. Our team was very close, practically inseparable. We spent hours eating together, laughing together and going out on the town together. Lane Alexander, Kate Ferris, Kamrin Purser (Rife), Leigh Furgson (Mays), Jennifer Clarkson, Jaime Oelke, and our trainer Lynn Tuller were some of my best friends and still are to this day.

Rollins volleyball team reunion, Beech Mtn., NC (2022)

As is typical, I decided to leave dorm life and move to greener pastures—a newly acquired condo building, now student housing. My favorite part about my move as I was about to start my junior year was that others from my volleyball team also decided to move into the same building. It was a spectacular disaster waiting to happen. Imagine 10 college volleyball players, all living in a beautiful condo building, all on the same floor. We all moved in, excited for the many nights (and days) to follow.

The funny thing is that the condo complex had been inhabited by older-aged residents, 55 and up, but our college had acquired it for student housing. One night, we realized that there were a few older folks still living on the floor where we lived! That did not change our impromptu idea to ride our bikes up and down the hallways. Bikes barreled down the hallway, with barely-restrained giggling filling the long corridor. Much to my surprise, a door opened and a small-framed, grey-haired woman stood still in sheer shock. I was riding tall on my Schwinn. After her sideways stare and a shaming scowl that would make any praying child cower, our team slunk back into our respective apartments, reeling from laughter. We sure gave that granny a true glimpse of college life.

My teammates and I would practice together, eat together, go out together, and even dressed up together for Halloween. One year, we all dressed up like Miss America Pageant contestants from the 1980s. Our neon blue eye shadow, shoulder pads, and over-crimped hair truly displayed the big splendor of the 1980s. Wearing draped sashes representing many states, we found a place to debut our look. A week before Halloween, we strolled into a club like we were on a red carpet—10 of us, with 5'9" being the average height of us divas.

Our premature costume presence shocked the club-goers as our overdone makeup and taffeta flared gowns did not quite fit in the trendy club. We didn't mind "making a scene," but I have to say that more people looked confused than impressed.

Miss Americas for Halloween (2001)

Playing on a college-level sports team has its perks, but it also has its hardships. While others were resting poolside after classes, we were obligated to attend afternoon workout sessions. They were hard. Our bodies were sore after playing at night, and our minds were tired with trying to balance schoolwork, homelife, personal life, and volleyball. This is how character grows deep roots—to be tired mentally is one thing, but to be tired mentally but also perform physically takes character.

Receiving continual feedback from our coach was also a character-building experience. Sometimes the feedback looked a little less like coaching and more like yelling in frustration for our inability to instantly correct or to constantly keep up a full-fledge effort. Like in the military, we could not talk back. We had to take coaching, yelling, pushing, tiredness, soreness—all of it with our heads held high, somehow mustering up confidence to put our best foot forward as we moved on. Playing volleyball in college and being under the microscope contributed a lot of the development of my resiliency.

I made it through all four years as a collegiate athlete, graduated, and started really thinking about what I wanted to do with my life. I realized my childhood dream of acting was probably not going to come to fruition. Law school? No, I couldn't take any more grueling schoolwork. I was done. I was eager and ready to join the real world and the workforce. I was outgoing, self-disciplined, and competitive—I decided to pursue a career in sales.

I applied for different positions and was even offered a job setting up events and traveling with a local company, but I declined. I had been waiting and hoping to be hired as a Medical Sales Representative. However, my plans were not my own and God had a different thing in store for me. I did not get the job with the medical company and had to humbly return to the event and marketing company to ask if they would still consider me for the position. They graciously said "yes" and I did not waste any time. I went from wearing a blue cap and gown at graduation to an Ann Taylor suit in a corporate building downtown the very next day. I was in shock.

My first day in corporate America was terrifying and exciting all at once. I sat in a window-filled conference room, overlooking our downtown area for Employee Orientation. I was wondering if what was happening was actually real. I felt sadness because I knew the time of adulthood had struck, but also excitement for my next chapter of life.

Shortly after this initial training, I began traveling and setting up events all over the country. I found a new life in this existence. I loved the busyness of it all; moving and going, traveling to new cities, hotels, places, and the people. I ate great food, stayed in some wonderful places and some not-so-nice places, and racked up over 200,000 air miles in less than two years. The passion for traveling was now a part of me.

Looking back, I realize how naïve I was, fearless and full of beginners' boldness. I wasn't really nervous about setting up large events in new cities. I made a lot of mistakes, but tried my best to roll with the opportunities. The job was so exciting, yet hard. I learned and polished my skills at public speaking because I often had to make introductions and lead meetings. I felt like I was doing the job of someone with 20-plus years' experience.

After two years, I made another big decision. I fell in love with San Diego in my travels (as many people do) and I decided to make the move. I loved my sunshine state of Florida, but it felt like sunny California was calling my name. I left my hometown to move across the country, living with two friends I had known from Florida. I did not yet have a job lined up. It was the first time in my life that I took what felt like a huge risk—leaving my well-paying job for a dream to live in California. I was excited, optimistic, and nervous all at the same time.

My move to California was not typical. I had everything planned out, but not in a traditional way. I did not announce it publicly or tell many people. I had done a lot of work many months prior to prepare myself for this huge and exciting change. With my living situation figured out in San Diego, I shipped boxes of clothes and such in advance and eventually sold my car in Florida. I was about to start my new life.

I flew into Los Angeles, not San Diego, initially. I had an interview set up with a medical company. I left the plane and headed to my rental car company, grabbed my keys and found my car. I went straight to the interview, which I thought went well, but I believe he sensed my indecisiveness and instability. He also knew my laissez-faire attitude about moving to Los Angles was a cover-up; I did not want to move to Los Angeles, and he knew it.

After the interview, I got into my rental car and it hit me. All the makings of my new life chapter-the excitement, the fear, the unknowns, the possibilities. I couldn't believe I was heading to San Diego, three hours away, and never looking back—not to Los Angeles, to Florida, to my family and friends. I was now a resident of California. When I got to San Diego, I was bursting with happiness. I had left it all to be there. Our apartment was two blocks from the beach. I could see the ocean from our balcony and walk to the beach in two minutes! It was everything I had ever wanted. Finally, I felt like I had made it.

The comradery and sisterhood between myself and my roommates were very reassuring. We worked out together, shopped together, cooked together, and had fun at the beach or anywhere we happened to be. They were my support system and made me feel like we were in this new adventure together. I cherished my times with them.

I loved being around other young people and doing fun things in a city most dream of living in. I met some incredible people including my best friends who all lived on the same street as we did. We would have "Sunday Fun-day" where we would watch football, eat and drink, hanging out the entire afternoon together. It was like one big happy family. Eventually I got a job with a large tradeshow company working with their exhibitors and helping set up exhibit halls. It was a fun job, but I was used to being in charge of events. I struggled being in such a junior position, not involved in making many decisions. However, co-workers like Alex Goldau made boring days fun. Alex's laid back and big perspective kept my spirits up. I worked at the tradeshow company for a few years and then made a change, accepting a job where I learned more than I could have ever hoped for.

The main boss, the Director, was super smart, but was always in "push mode." While we would be working on one project, she would have four more projects lined up. She was always ten steps ahead of us. I learned more from her about business than I did from anyone else. I worked as a Marketing Project Manager, helping manage all the internal events including tradeshows, annual conferences, employee events, and more. It was a great job, but demanding. I struggled to keep up at times, but my direct Manager was very helpful and guided me to staying on track.

While work was going well, so was my personal life. Out one night in a dark downtown club, I bellied up to the bar to order my usual cocktail, vodka cranberry. While waiting for the overworked female bartender to glance my way, I noticed a good-looking guy standing fairly close to me. He was also waiting for a drink with friends. We made eye contact and starting discussing the ins and outs of bar life—waiting for a simple drink, the overpriced drinks at some places versus other places, and the typical lack of air conditioning in places such as this. We laughed at ourselves as we instantly became the Siskel and Ebert of bar life.

As the night continued on, we did, too. We laughed and talked, eventually exchanging contact information. As I slipped into a car filled with friends, I got a text from the great guy at the bar, thanking me for a fun time. That man later became my daughter's father.

He and I dated, enjoying nights out for sushi and movie nights filled with funny films making us laugh until our bellies hurt. He was a wonderful man, in the Navy, and incredibly fun. I enjoyed my time with him. Life was going very well.

Everything changed, though. After he decided not to re-enlist, this man I had been spending all my free time with and had grown to love, decided to move home to Oklahoma. He didn't have much choice, he felt. I sensed that our lives were coming to a fork in the road, two different paths ahead. He chose a place that felt familiar, a place to settle down, and I chose San Diego, a place with new opportunities and many friends to meet. When he moved away, we stayed in touch; however, we did our own things in our respective places of residence. He shared about new loves, new adventures, and all the things close friends would talk about, and I shared about the same, maybe at times a little more exciting! He was as much a part of my life as a best friend. Then I met another man who was in the military, fell in love, and was having the time of my life.

We traveled to music shows, enjoyed running races and fun nights outs. This man helped me truly enjoy all that the West Coast had to offer until one day when it all suddenly changed. His duty station changed him to the coast of North Carolina where he would be deployed overseas for 18 months. I was devastated. I didn't know what to do.

I decided to leave San Diego and move to live with my amazing family in the mountains of North Carolina. It was hard to imagine leaving San Diego, but I wanted to be closer to him so that once he returned from overseas, we could continue where we left off. Yet, as time would tell, it didn't work out that way. He and I didn't happen. He left for overseas and I was left hanging. I lived in a town so different than San Diego, struggling to fit in or know my purpose. I was floundering. I knew there was more to life than just small jobs and living in my sister's basement, but I didn't know what.

Family, Franklin, NC (2021)

I started to adjust, taking in all that Western North Carolina had to offer, eventually moving into a "tiny house," where I enjoyed hiking trails, cooking outdoors, painting on weekend nights, and living a simple life. I started to *find my place* again. The ocean was my first love, but the mountains began to hold a very special place in my heart, also. I was slowly slipping into a new normal until one day, my best friend from Oklahoma mentioned that he was coming to visit me. I was excited to have him come and see all that I had discovered about the beautiful mountains and their amazing people. He made the trip to North Carolina and our feelings soon flourished from friendship to more—true love. I was happy, but afraid. This little peaceful life I had created for myself was now being interrupted by an incredible human being, but I didn't know how it would all work. I had so many questions.

Would he leave his home state to join me in the mountains? Would things work this time? Were we really on the same page about the simple things in life? Time would quickly prove that he was determined to make things work, make US work…so he asked me to marry him. I will never forget that day.

I had flown to Oklahoma to see him and where he had grown up. It was early in the evening, and I was cooking Pad Thai for dinner. I stood in the kitchen of his small Oklahoma house and he came in, staring at me. He said something goofy, then, with a beautiful ring in hand, asked me to marry him. He forgot the kneeling down part, but we just laughed. It was so us! I said "yes" and together, our life planning began.

We talked about where we would live, what kind of house we would buy, where I could work, what he would do for work, how many children we would have…the dreaming went on and on and I had never been more excited in my life. My dreams of being a wife and mother finally were coming true. I was so happy and my thoughts were so clear.

More Than "I'm Sorry"

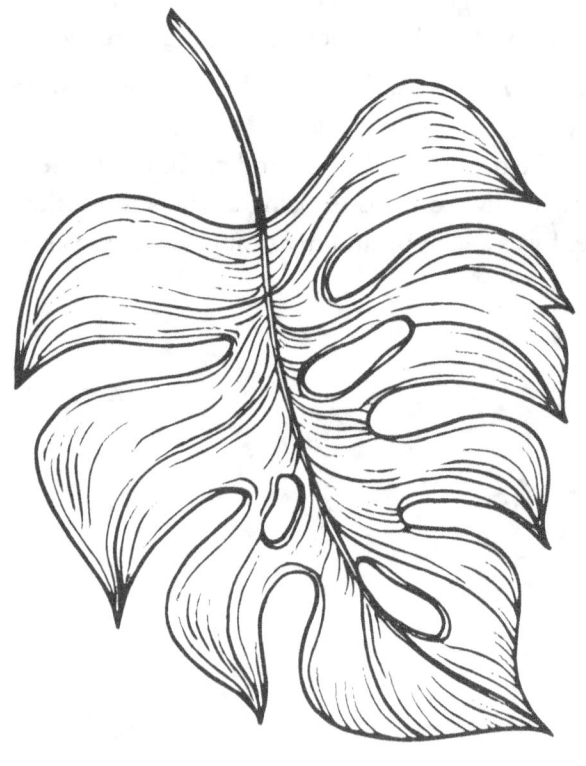

CHAPTER 2

Painting a Beautiful Future

It was a gorgeous day in May, 2013, and we were in the mountains of Western North Carolina/North Georgia. The chairs lined the green grass of a golf course event lawn. Grass-covered steps led up to a large pergola covered in vines and with a chandelier dripping in glass pieces. This was our wedding day. Spirits were high and family and friends started filling seats. The music started and the wedding party started stepping down nature's aisle. I stood with my father, surrounded by mountains, looking over the wedding guests. It was our time next.

My father walked me down the aisle and my brother stood waiting with my husband and the others in the wedding party. My brother performed the ceremony. It was all so surreal. After the ceremony, we held a reception at a family member's historical home, built in the early 1900s. We danced, ate food, and had fun. I couldn't have been happier. My new husband and I left that night for our honeymoon cruise. I couldn't believe I had married my best friend and life was actually working out beautifully.

When the honeymoon was over, we were both a little unprepared for reality. We had planned to live in North Carolina in my tiny house for the short-term, but my husband wasn't able to convince his company to let him work remotely. He couldn't live in North Carolina, or anywhere but Oklahoma. We had to do things much differently than I wanted.

I had to leave all I knew, all I built, to join him in Oklahoma in his small, not-so-glamourous house. I didn't want to leave my family, friends, church, job or house. I didn't want to leave the mountains for the not-so-alluring state of Oklahoma. I was sad and felt very depressed. However, as a good and accommodating wife, I swallowed my true feelings, packed up my things, and left for Oklahoma with my husband.

It was not easy. The simple, easy-going life I had created was no longer what life looked life. I had to adjust all over again, all the while dealing with a new marriage. We struggled some financially as a lot of new marriages do, but found ways to have fun and enjoy life's simplicities. It was a hot summer Saturday and we decided that this day was the day to "splurge." We had been talking about a kiddie pool for our bare backyard and we finally decided to purchase one. We went to the local big box store and bought one for $25. We then made ice cold lemonades and went in the pool as though we were in the Grand Cayman Islands. Those were good days and we had more of those than not.

We starting meeting friends from church and got into a rhythm. Work life was strange as it was one of the first times in my life that I didn't have a job. My husband was still working for the company he worked for when we got married, which caused him to travel around the state quite often. I eventually started accompanying and assisting him; his work took him to rural county courthouses. We would get up early each morning, make our hot cups of coffee, and hit the road. Fields of corn filled the horizon for miles, and I often wondered, *who lives in rural places like this?* I had never seen so few houses on so many fields and farms.

We worked in some of the smallest towns I had ever seen, where Dollar Generals served as the main shopping venue. We would enter courthouses, set up our photography equipment, and begin filming documents. My husband would digitize records for the oil and gas industry so everything could be viewed electronically. It was certainly a market I never knew about, but one that made sense after seeing how rural the courthouses were. Most companies would not want to send a team to these places to gather deed and record information, so my husband served as the researcher and collector of data for various companies.

Eventually, he went out on his own, pursuing record digitization full time, under his own company name. This work led us to Kansas, where he won a large job digitizing a huge number of deed books in a town outside of Wichita. It was an extremely small town, with one large box store and one street filled with locally-owned shops. It was a special place, though.

The Wellington Kansas people welcomed us with open arms as we moved into a large, 1920s corner house with a wooden porch wrapping the entire front. We loved that house. We found a church, connected with the youth, and started really enjoying the courthouse work. Life was simple again. We didn't know how long the job would take, but we worked hard together daily in order to finish and move onto another job. I was conflicted because I really liked our home and all that the little town had done for us as a couple. And we were really growing and learning about each other. We walked each night, strolling along the town's streets, looking at the old homes, dreaming and picturing what life was like *back then*. Sunday nights became Chinese food nights and Tuesday nights were my dance class nights with Miss Michelle. I felt happy.

My joy grew more than I ever knew it could when in November of 2012, I started to feel a little strange right around dinnertime. I enjoyed cooking and planning meals and this one particular night, I had made crockpot chicken, fresh vegetables, and a Caesar salad for our dinner. I went to serve the chicken and immediately got sick. I really wasn't thinking much of it, but soon realized I might be pregnant. My husband and I went to the store to get pregnancy tests. We scanned the aisles for just the right one and landed on a "Clear Blue." We brought the tests home and headed to our bathroom. I closed the door and was shaking as I took the test. He waited outside the door. I looked down and saw the plus sign. I was shocked. *Could this be real?* It was that cold November night in 2012 that I found out the greatest news I had ever known—I was pregnant.

All the things that typically happen once a woman finds out she is expecting started to happen. I spent hours researching the baby's development, shopping for all things baby, and figuring out what name would be ours for our little girl or boy.

Looking back, I realize that an expecting mom's daydreams don't stop with creating a birthing plan, welcoming a boy or a girl, and calling them by their name for the first time. The child is inserted into a mother's forever future even before she lays eyes on her baby. Scenes from their future life together fill her head, everything from seeing her Christmas cards become child-with-Santa ones to wondering if the dad's musical talent will be passed on as one of her child's gifts. If she is already a mother, she's thinking about the wonderful sibling bond she'll nurture and how one day her children's children will be close cousin-friends who play in her back yard. There's a vividly imagined lifetime, a whole new world that feels real, once a mother gives her own flesh and blood to create a new little human.

Things were going well the first few months as we prepared to have our little one. We were finishing up our job at the Kansas courthouse and discussing where to go next. Should we move to North Carolina and enjoy the mountains? We knew we couldn't stay in Kansas as there weren't any more jobs for us, and we agreed on the idea of Asheville, North Carolina. With our baby coming, it would be great to be close to my family.

I began looking for homes to move into near Asheville and found a quaint home outside the city on a small piece of land. A duck-filled pond and budding trees filled the mountain landscape. I was excited to have some space to roam and a new beginning. I had my family drive over to view the home and take pictures. I was set on that house. We completed the application and were approved to rent the home.

I could not wait to move into our cute, country oasis. My husband continued to pursue courthouse jobs and various digitizing opportunities in the Western North Carolina area. The opportunities seemed endless and I was excited for the work that he could do to support our growing family. There were many things to be excited about: our new home in the country, living near an incredible city filled with culture, great food, and family—and mostly, the upcoming birth of our sweet little one.

Our plan was to pack up our home in late February of 2013, drive across the country, and move into our new home. We were on our way to making all of this happen when I got the call that changed everything.

CHAPTER 3

No Words

I sat on our couch in our oversized 1920s living room in Wellington, Kansas, staring at how under-decorated our rental home looked. We needed more furniture. I longed for a "homey" feeling.

My family had called to tell me news about my dad. Things were not good. My emotions ran through my body and I felt frozen. I never knew how I would feel if my dad were to ever get sick or need surgery, but now, in this moment, his mortality was in my face. I had feared deep down that my dad would die before friends' dads because he was so much older, but I never wanted that day to come. I felt frozen in the heavy words that were stuck in my mind, "Dad needs surgery."

Dad had been admitted into the local hospital in a small town outside where they lived in North Carolina and would need surgery on his foot. He had gangrene from poor circulation. *My poor, sweet daddy*, I thought. My heart ached for him, but I didn't know what to do with my dad being hurt, sick, or "not okay." It was my greatest nightmare.

The thing about my dad was that he was active, playing golf, working almost every day; yet, he was somehow now sick, needing a surgery no one knew about? *How could this be?* This was all new to me and shocking for everyone.

My husband and I decided that I would fly to Asheville right then, two weeks ahead of the moving truck that my husband would drive across the country. The timing was strange. We were set to start our new life, but everything started changing.

I landed in Asheville and my sister drove me to the hospital. Gloom filled the air and the green trees of the mountain line I grew up knowing didn't feel familiar. It all felt strange. The fog laid thick, and I was concerned. Finally at the hospital, I walked into my dad's 8x10 stark room and saw him lying there. It was dark and there were no lights on. I felt like I was living someone else's life because I certainly didn't comprehend what was going on.

Hearing the crinkling sounds of the plastic mattress as I sat on his bed, I noticed that I was very, very scared. I tried to calm my voice as I said, "Dad? It's me."

He opened his eyes and said, "Noelley? How did you get here?" For a moment, he seemed okay. He seemed to know who I was, but he was foggy. He asked, "Where's your mother? My sweetie-pie?"

"She's coming. She's in the hallway." My dad seemed somewhat himself, but I then saw the first thing I can ever remember as causing my dad physical pain—his foot. It was wrapped in white, bandaged from the ankle to the ends of his toes, but where his big toe should be, there was a shocking gap. A space was open that his once-perfect toe had filled. I later learned that, because of his diabetes, he had sustained such a bad infection that his toe had to be amputated. It was heart-breaking. There lay my dad in that hospital bed, missing a toe and in pain. I was in shock. A wave of sadness came over me. This man, my knight in shining armor, was no longer perfect. His little princess saw him for what he was—mortal. I was so sad, but that was only the beginning of what was to come.

The medical team decided that he needed to be transported to the larger Asheville hospital for more testing on his heart, as they feared he may have had a stroke during the amputation surgery. I agreed that the larger hospital with more access and staff would be best. We waited for hours (which seemed like forever) until the ambulance and transportation team finally arrived. My mom rode along, with me driving, following the ambulance to the larger hospital, about 20 miles away. All of a sudden, the ambulance pulled away and starting racing at such a high speed that I couldn't keep up. I began shaking.

I drove as fast as I could, eventually arriving at the hospital. We hurried down hallways that, in my memories, were endless. We rode up the slowest elevator in the world to the floor where he should have been. He was not there. "Your dad was taken straight to the Emergency Room as there was an incident in the ambulance," said one of the nurses at the nurse's station, barely looking up.

With panic and fear filling us, we went back down the elevator and entered a maze of hallways, eventually finding the ER. We were met by another nurse who escorted us to a small empty room. I started panicking. This was like a room I had never really seen other than on *Grey's Anatomy* or a *Dateline* episode. It was a private room for private talk. The nurse stood in the doorway and he said a line now embedded in my mind: "A chaplain is going to come speak to you."

A chaplain? Why a chaplain? I wanted to run into a field screaming. My brain couldn't keep up with my emotions. I couldn't think straight. It was one of the first times in my existence that I felt an inability to order my thoughts. They were running rampant and I was feeling out of control. We had no idea what was going on or what had happened to my precious dad. We waited anxiously in the stark, impersonal room for someone—anyone—to come and relieve a moment of our anxiety-stricken thoughts. The chaplain and ER physician finally came in. They sat down with us, opening their mouths to tell us news I wasn't ready to hear. "Your dad suffered a heart attack in the ambulance and things are not good." *That explains the speed,* I began to rationalize.

The waves of emotions crashed. Everything stopped swirling and crashed hard on the shore of my soul. My life, my incredible childhood, my sweet daddy. Everything was moving both faster and slower than I wanted. I opened my mouth to speak, to ask how this could be possible, but no words would come out. I thought I was going to pass out. Then, coming into focus, I heard, "Do you want to go back and see him?" We stood up.

Walking through the double doors, seeing machines and wired-covered people, I couldn't believe what I was doing. I looked ahead to see my dad lying there, covered to his chin in a blanket, with a tube in his mouth, and I started sobbing. *How could this be? How could my dad not be okay?* I was only 32 years old!

The next few hours were a blur. We sat in the main ER waiting room, unaware of all the emergencies coming in. Ours was the only one we cared about. They ended up wheeling Dad up to the Intensive Care Unit and we followed. The long hallways seemed even longer and I wanted so badly for a snap of my fingers to make it all better. We waited in the ICU waiting room, where a nurse and ICU intensivist greeted us. They shared my dad's condition was not good and that they would be working to keep him stable. We prayed, we cried, we struggled with the "why."

The Palliative Care team wanted to meet with us. I didn't even know what they did or who they were. I had never dealt with so many people in one place before. With clipboards in hand, which they used to reference my father's name, they had us gather in a circle. The room was like a prison—no character, no color, just plain and cold. They didn't seem to care about my dad, but instead were more concerned about giving us their opinion so they could move onto their next patient. They shared that my dad needed open heart surgery and that it could be very risky. I was mad. I did not like them. *How could they talk about my dad, my hero, like he was a science experiment or some expired item needing to be discarded?* They sat, with their white coats and clipboards, waiting for our answer. Our family went out and talked, then decided that we would proceed with the heart surgery. We had to. He would want us to.

My father needed five bypasses to repair his heart. He came out of surgery and we were all on pins and needles, hoping and praying for the best. He started recovering very well physically, but he was disoriented and it was obvious his mind was not fully recovered. He knew who some of us were, but he did not know basic information about the hospital, his doctors, nor remember some of his friends that had visited. It was all so strange to me. He'd had the memory of steel trap. It was very hard to see him falter, to not be able to put two and two together. We tried to brush it off as being the anesthesia and all the medication. My dad ultimately did not get better. He had complication after complication and sadly, his body gave out.

I sat by his bedside and watched my father die. It all happened too fast. I was then escorted out to my sister's car to leave the mountain town hospital and head towards her home. I sat in the passenger's seat gazing out the front large window, wondering if the driving would make things better.

I felt the most intense pain in my heart that I had ever felt in all of my life. I didn't know if being anywhere or with anyone would help me. It all felt like too much.

Linnie & John Moore, Franklin, NC (2011)

Not All Loss and Grief is the Same

An insurmountable amount pain landed five months later. I was introduced to a pain much different, and sadly, much more intense—the loss of my only child. There were so many things that made the loss feel more intense, much sharper, with a cruel and ragged edge. In the next chapter, I share the story of my daughter who died less than four weeks after being born. Forgive me if the pages are tear-stained.

The thing is, nothing prepares a mother for that life-altering, nature-opposing event—nothing at all. Like a rock ripped out from under winding weeds and dirt, I was suddenly exposed to terrifying elements I was not ready for.

With a father or mother, as well as grandparents or older folks, most people have an awareness of their fragility. I did. I knew as my parents grew older, there would be a day I wouldn't be able to call and ask for business advice or hang out with them at Sunday dinners. I knew that when an elderly person at our church was admitted to the hospital, it was not unusual for them to never come home.

When I was in seventh grade, our music teacher taught us pieces to sing for older folks in an assisted living home. As young teenagers, we didn't understand why this mattered or what the significance was; we did it because it was required for a good grade. Our class met in the lobby of a two-story, bricked-covered assisted living home, where a mashed potato smell filled the air. I was uncomfortable and scared to be there as it was all so new for me.

Our class lined up in perfect form to share our tried-and-true songs. The residents were pushed in or shuffled in to listen. As it started to become more real to me, I was becoming overwhelmed. Then I looked up at the front row to see a sweet-faced older man in a wheelchair, who looked just like my dad. Hot tears started sliding down my face and I realized that my heart always had an awareness that my parents would grow older and older and someday not be with me, but I had to stuff it down.

It broke my heart that day to see that man who looked like my dad, but with more wrinkles. Nature prepares us for our older loved ones' departure by showing us many signs—their looks change, they slow down, their mind wanders. It's a natural process.

However, nature plays a cruel joke on many with the loss of a child. There is no time to even contemplate life's fragility because the days are filled with hope, joy, and exciting anticipation. Expectant parents live dream-filled days. *Will my son play baseball? Will my daughter have a turned-up nose like her grandmother? Will my daughter love to sing? Will she enjoy science? What special bond will my son have with his big brother?*

And then, if the child dies, both the present and the future are abruptly and permanently shattered.

This is perhaps the most incomprehensible pain to understand when you see a grieving parent. Not only did their small child die, but so did the enormous, far-reaching future of infinite possibilities that they have been imagining. Reality itself has been destroyed.

Understandably, this grief can be paralyzing. The human heart and brain are seemingly unable to move when the natural order of birth, life, and death get jumbled. Losing a child makes a person in motion, moving through the days of life, stand still.

"The death of a child is considered the single worst stressor a person can go through," explains Deborah Carr, chair of the sociology department at Boston University. "Parents…feel responsible for the child's well-being. So when they lose a child, they're not just losing a person they loved. They're also losing the years of promise they had looked forward to."

A woman who loses her husband is a "widow." A man whose wife dies is a "widower." A child that has lost their parents is an "orphan." For a mother or father who survives the death of their child, there are no words.

From personal experience, I know that people often mistakenly assume that an infant's life was so short that it must be easier to grieve an infant dying than other types of losses. However, the truth is quite opposite. Losing an infant, who didn't get to live out their life and whose parents held big dreams and hopes dearly, feels like a huge and tragic loss—and the heartache is impossible to soothe with "a long life of good memories."

The pain is amplified with the sense of feeling robbed. A parent can't understand why an innocent child was robbed of their chance at life. A parent feels they were also robbed of all the years of loving their child, showing them their first *everything*, watching them grow into precious little original personalities.

Many parents also have an overwhelming sense of guilt. Everyone in the world knows that a parent's primary role is to protect their child. It's in our human DNA to ensure the survival of our offspring. The guilt for moms is sometimes her feeling that her own body failed. She didn't build a healthy baby. She didn't do something she was supposed to do. The father feels like a failure in similar ways. The parents torment themselves with what they could have and should have done. Guilt is one of the most debilitating emotions parents must deal with after the loss of an infant.

Is this guilt warranted? I personally don't know any mothers who smoked crack or otherwise abused their pregnant bodies. The moms I know are conscientious during their baby's development, wanting to be as healthy as possible for the baby's sake. She attends pre-natal appointments, takes her super-vitamins and long walks, researches how to care for a child, and asks friends and family endless parenting questions. A mother prepares for her mothering role much further out than only when a child is inside her womb.

After my daughter Finley Elizabeth entered the world and then died before her one-month birthday, guilt consumed me on many levels. I felt guilty that I didn't know she was potentially suffering. I felt guilty that I had chosen a doctor who apparently cared more about her vacation than about Finley and me. I felt guilty about using a hospital which didn't provide full-time obstetrics coverage. And finally, I felt an excruciating level of guilt that I didn't follow my own motherly instinct that something was wrong. I should have been MUCH more assertive. I felt broken and inadequate as a mother. Ultimately, I felt responsible for my daughter's death.

Years have gone by and countless therapy sessions have unraveled much of my guilt, but at first, it was one of the most dominant emotions, second to anger, that I had to work through. I had to grab onto tools to stop the sometimes-broken cycle of blame, guilt, and anger. I often had flashbacks of the day she died, how she died, and my *inability to do anything* to save her. The trauma around losing a child, the one thing on earth that is truly ours, can be devastating emotionally, physiologically, and physically.

Kristen Fuller, M.D. writes in *Psychology Today* (online): "Although parents mourning the loss of a child are, in many ways, experiencing classic grief responses—the usual battery of psychological, biological, and social repercussions—there are many unique challenges. The trauma is often more intense, the memories and hopes harder to let go of. As such, the mourning process is longer...

"One surprising impact, often seen among parents mourning the loss of a child, is known as the broken-heart syndrome—a condition that presents oddly like a textbook heart attack. Symptoms include "crushing chest, pain, ST-segment elevation on electrocardiography, and elevated cardiac enzyme markers on lab results," Fuller said, citing her previously written work on the subject.

Yes, she is right. "Broken-heart syndrome" is a descriptive way for others to gain at least a little understanding of this kind of grief. The death and loss of a child is frequently called the ultimate tragedy. Along with the usual symptoms and stages of grief, there are many issues that make parental bereavement particularly difficult to resolve. As I discussed earlier, the grief can be exacerbated and complicated by feelings of injustice—the understandable feeling that this loss never should have happened.

During the early days of grieving, most parents have alternating experiences of excruciating pain and numbness—a dichotomy that may persist for months or longer. Many parents who have lost their son or daughter report they feel that they can only "exist" and every motion or need beyond that seems nearly impossible. It has been said that coping with the death and loss of a child requires some of the hardest work one will ever have to do. That is certainly true for myself and other moms I have helped.

In summary, to become a compassionate and effective helper to a parent who lost a child, you must give up your old definitions of grieving the loss of a loved one. This is different. Unless you've experienced losing a child, you cannot know, so don't imagine that you do. Once, a well-meaning person said to me, "I know exactly how you feel. My grandmother died on the same day as your baby." This had the opposite effect than being of comfort to me.

A mother told me her lifelong friend did not reach out to her after her child died. She wondered for two years how this could be, since another friend said she had told the woman when it happened. Two years later, the still-grieving mom called her friend who said, "I just didn't know what to say. I couldn't call you because I had no words." The mom told her that she would have appreciated a call or letter that said "I have no words. I love you." The point is that no one has the right consoling and comforting words, because there are none. It's okay to not know what to say.

Here is what you CAN know: everything suggested in the following chapters of this book. Years of experience and dedicated immersion in helping mothers who are grieving the loss of a child have given me the keys to unlock real-world solutions for helping. The mom doesn't need you to feel the pain that they feel, they need you to help them get through it. Start by relieving them from having to think, trying to use their knotted-up mind jungle.

In the back of this book, I have included the exact Model and Steps that have been proven to work in the wake of this unique tragedy. These are the difference-making points you can learn and act on without hesitation. I have also developed a separate, complete "Care Guide" for anyone who would find a handy workbook-type guide helpful as they endeavor to help a grieving mother.

But first, it is my bittersweet honor to tell you about Finley Elizabeth.

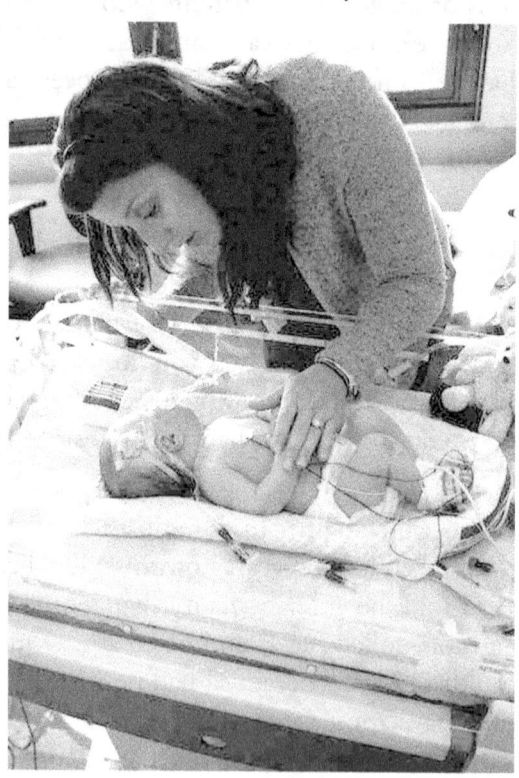

Noelle & Finley, Hospital (2013)

CHAPTER 4

My Daughter

I went into my OBGYN's office for my 39-week checkup and my husband joined me. We sat in the 1990's style waiting room, laughing and talking about how scary it was that we were going to be parents. It was a frightening talk. We were called to the back area by a nurse and the measuring began. First, weight: only 19 pounds gained since beginning of pregnancy; then height, 5'11 as usual; then blood pressure, normal as can be. We were then escorted into the darkened room where the sonograms take place. I had to hoist up onto the crinkly-papered table to then have the sonographer pour cold goop all over my belly. It made me laugh. We couldn't wait to hear the heartbeat.

Doppler ultrasound uses sound waves to detect the movement of blood in vessels. It is used in pregnancy to study blood circulation in the baby, uterus, and placenta. There is a speaker that projects the sound out of the womb. Slowly, she moved the Doppler around, and we heard it! A strong, pulsating heartbeat like 50 kindergarteners running through a hallway. We were so excited. The sonographer wiped the goop off and I sat up in shear elation. All was good!

We waited and waited, but the doctor was running really behind and my husband had to leave for work. I sat there on the crinkly paper sheet, feeling as if all my underlings were showing in the too-small paper coverup. Waiting for the doctor. Finally, the door opened, and 8 words came out of her mouth, "Are you ready to have a baby today?" I was shocked and immediately got nervous. I couldn't believe what was happening or what she was saying.

I said, "Sure, I guess."

She said, "You guess?"

"Well, of course, but why?"

"Well, you don't really have a choice," the doctor said. "Your amniotic fluid is low and she needs to be delivered."

Fear and uncertainty led to a deluge of questions pouring forth. "Do I need to go by ambulance? Is she in danger? Is this urgent? What needs to be done right now?" My mama bear instinct had kicked in.

"No," she said, "you don't have to go by ambulance, and you can even go home to grab your things, but don't spend a lot of time at home."

I was whirling with excitement edged with nervousness. I couldn't believe my time had come, but I felt alone and scared. I started crying because I couldn't believe I heard that news by myself. That's when a wave of panic overcame me. I walked out of the doctor's office, got in my car and started to try and call people. I couldn't seem to dial the phone fast enough. I called my mom, then my husband, then my sister-in-law.. I was afraid. I tried to tell them what was going on through tears filling my eyes because I didn't quite understand what was happening. My husband said he would come home right away and get me.

I pulled into my driveway and went inside to methodically grab the things I had prepared in advance. My mind seemed like a blob. I couldn't process what was happening. Finally, my husband arrived home in a panic. I could tell her was scared too. It wasn't a typical delivery; it was because of the low amniotic fluid. That is what seemed to be making us afraid, plus the anxiety of being first-time parents.

At 1:15 p.m., I climbed into our car as he loaded the infant car seat into the back. I couldn't believe this was happening. We started driving to our local hospital and the rain started. In no time, it was pouring so hard we could barely see. The sky was completely grey, which made the summer day seem gloomy compared to the normally bright Florida sunshine. The oak-lined street of the town I was born in seemed so familiar, but so foreign. Everything felt scary and strange.

We got to the hospital approximately 14 minutes after leaving our house and pulled up into valet. I couldn't believe it—we were going to have a baby. We walked into the hospital and went up the elevator. We checked in and were told to wait in the seating area. So, we sat. Eventually my mom arrived, and we all talked about what our baby girl's middle name would be. "Would you like her middle name to be named after you, Mom? Linn? Or after Elizabeth?"

Mom said, "You should name he Finley Elizabeth, after your sister. That has a much better ring to it then Finley Linn." We all laughed, enjoying the light-hearted distraction from the serious purpose of this family get-together.

Shortly after this name discussion, we were called back. It was around 3 p.m. The hallway was busy with task-focused nurses as we followed one into our room. We were all looking around. We noticed the cute little bed ready for our daughter, along with a small brush, nail clippers, and nose cleaner. We started to make ourselves comfortable. We put her Baby Book in that bed, open so that her footprints could be placed in the book.

The nurse began prepping me, handing me the soft blue coverup to be tied in the back. Such a strange thing. I went into the bathroom, removed my low-fashion maternity clothes, stepped into the "gown" and pulled it up my arms, having my husband tie the neck and back. After a few steps back to the bed, I sat down and the Doppler was then placed on my belly.

Sitting there so exposed with only the inadequate coverup, I laughed, making some joke about how small the coverup was and my mom and husband chuckled, too. The nurse checked my vitals and everything was good. Around 5 p.m., my OBGYN and her new physician partner walked in. She introduced me to the woman who "may end up helping along the way." I felt myself flinch as I was hit with this news. I did not know that my doctor had a new partner, and had never met her. I felt weird, but accepted it, because of the common notion that "zillions of women have been having babies since the dawn of time." I felt like I should just go along with everything as routine, something others knew all about and I, the rookie, knew nothing about.

The doctor spoke with me about the plan for the upcoming next few hours—induction. They planned on giving me Pitocin and then would apply pharmacologic agents to ripen my cervix if things did not progress. All sounded good to me. It started to feel real that Finley would be coming over the next few hours and I was terrified, but thrilled! I couldn't wait.

At approximately 7 p.m., on July 24, I began receiving Pitocin through an IV in my arm to induce labor. I was told I would start to feel contractions. I waited in anticipation, not knowing what contractions would actually feel like. My husband, mom, and now also my sister-in-law were hanging out. Over the next few hours, I did not feel much of anything.

When night began to fall, everything started to slow down. My doctors left the hospital and nurses came in less frequently. Around 1 a.m., only my husband remained in the room with me as my painful contractions started. He was sound asleep, which I found annoying and thought, *must be nice*.

Shortly after 2 a.m., a nurse I hadn't seen before came in to check on me. She was too energetic for the time of night, moving things about quickly, roughly and loudly. She informed me that she would be adding cervical ripening medicine since I wasn't progressing as I should. I was scared, but had no idea what was about to ensue. The nurse took the medication and pushed it in a place inside my body I didn't know existed. I shrieked in pain. My husband finally woke up. I wanted to hit her. She had said it may hurt some, but I shouldn't feel it. That was a lie. I felt sick it hurt so much.

She left and I was still in pain, tears pouring from my eyes. My husband was the last person who could answer, but I bombarded him with, "What did she do to me? What was that? Why did I need that?"

Shortly after she left, I started to feel pulsating cramps and an aching that I hadn't felt before. It seemed like she had ripped something or torn something. Over the next five hours, I rolled from side to side in pain. Periodically, the night nurse checked on me, assuring me that the medication I'd received would help the labor progress. I was so upset with her, nothing she said reassured or helped me at all. She was *done*, in my book.

At 4 a.m., an anesthesiologist came into the room to check on me. He asked about the pain level. I told him it was VERY high since the Cervidil. He asked, "Do you want an epidural?" I wasn't sure if that was the right thing or if this was the right time, but I didn't know when the right time would be—I just wanted the pain to subside. He proceeded to prep my back and had me sitting up. He applied a cool sort of liquid and had me sit VERY still. I did. He injected the needle into my spine, and I felt a cool, tingling sensation running down my torso into my legs. I felt numb. I felt relief.

He gathered his things and had me sit back after some time. He asked how I was feeling, and I said, "Much better."

I laid my head down and got a few hours' sleep, but woke to a bright eastern sun shining. Finally, the sunny morning had arrived, and I had never been so happy to see it in my entire life. The night's terrors and pains seemed to dissipate as the light grew brighter. A new day had arrived. I knew my baby girl was about to come and this day, July 25, would be her birthday!

The morning brought new energy and people moving about. Thankfully, it brought a new team of nurses. It was early morning and I still hadn't seen my OBGYN or her new partner. I wondered why, but assumed it was just "normal" to only see the nursing staff up to this point. I did not know what to expect and I felt myself getting more and more anxious as hours went by.

Mid-morning, my obstetrician made her appearance. Her new partner was not with her. She asked how the night shift went. I shared how horrific the cervix treatment had been and that no one had warned me. She asked about how the epidural was doing, and I said "amazing." After her exam, she said that I was dilated only three centimeters, and we would just continue see how things progressed. I didn't really understand why everything was taking so long, but I believed that she would of course know what was happening and the best course of action.

Why, I wondered later, was I so okay with going along with everything the doctor has said? I wish I hadn't blindly trusted so much. I wished I had spoken up to ask more questions. I had a strange and unsettled gut feeling, not understanding why things were taking so long. But I pushed those thoughts aside and simply trusted the doctor. I was the one who had never done this before; she was the experienced authority.

Morning was moving along and friends were filling my phone with text messages. Everyone was excited, including me! My husband and I talked about the weeks to come and how things would be. We planned and prepped, laughing at many of the unknowns. My mom came to be there, right by my side, along with my sister-in-law and brother. My other sister was on her way from North Carolina.

At 12 noon, my obstetrician arrived to check my cervix. I was still only dilated 3-4 centimeters, even after being on 15 hours of Pitocin. My sister-in-law was starting to vocalize her concern. She asked the doctor what the plan was and was told that things were progressing as they should. She did not seem satisfied with that answer and I got nervous. I asked the obstetrician again, "So we do this for how long?" She said that she could do a C-section (surgery on my abdomen to remove the baby), but that it was not necessary or ideal this early on. I trusted her. So, my OBGYN left the room, leaving us feeling uneasy. I tried to stay focused on her words, "…this is normal, this is okay."

Then it was mid-afternoon. I was fortunate to have family there with me for distraction, sharing stories, fond memories, and future plans. Friends were texting, wondering if sweet Finley had made her appearance yet. Nothing had happened.

At 5 p.m., my OBGYN and her partner entered my room to check on me. She checked my cervix, concluding the same thing—not much progression, only four to five centimeters. She told the (nice) nurse to move me from side to side, rotating my body from right to left. We practiced for a bit, but it was hard and very uncomfortable. Almost 20 hours had gone by at this point, being on Pitocin, and everyone was getting tense. I didn't understand what was going on and why things were taking forever. I was assured that the baby was okay, and all was going well. It was a "normal labor."

Then she informed me she was leaving for vacation. Right then. Her new partner would be taking over my care. I felt a wave of sheer panic come over me. And I was mad. *Why would my doctor leave me? Why wasn't she doing anything? How could she just leave me with a stranger?* I was upset, to say the least. Stunned, I said nothing.

She did leave, and the new partner stayed. She talked with me for a few minutes and then, turned to leave. I couldn't believe it and felt abandoned. I couldn't believe they wouldn't hurry things along or stay with me until Finley came into the world.

Around 6 p.m., both OBGYN partners left the hospital, and that's when my life changed forever.

My Daughter

I waited. And waited. And waited, thinking that any second, the OBGYN I'd been handed off to would come into the room and *some* next step would begin.

The nurse was doing what the doctor had asked, having me turn periodically from one side to the next, supposedly to help move labor along. At 7 p.m., an hour after we started, I rolled to my left side and asked the nurse if I could lay flat. I was very uncomfortable. She said that I could, and it was not a problem. The nurse left the room.

Thirty minutes later, she came rushing into my room. She wasn't seeing anything on the fetal monitor on the nurses' station screens, so she came in to adjust the Doppler. She seemed calm, but very intent. However, moments later, chaos ensued. She called for others to come in and help her. She was unable to find Finley's heartbeat; she kept trying and trying. They decided to insert an internal monitor and were gathering the tubing to do so.

Panic permeated the room. I was nearly hyperventilating with anxiety. The nurse manger located the tubing for the internal fetal monitor, and she placed it inside. Still, very little activity on the monitor. Another nurse threw scrubs at my husband and told him to come with her, but then she quickly said, "Forget it, we don't have time."

All of a sudden, a nurse yelled, "We got to go." They quickly yanked the bed handles up, disconnected the Pitocin drip, and *started running* with my bed rolling down the hallway. The landscape paintings on the walls were a blur as I was rushed past. All the while, I was crying. I was so scared. I saw so many faces staring at me, many full of concern. At one point, someone tried to hand me paperwork to sign; another nurse yelled and said not to do that.

I was whisked through a door with the sign, "Operating Room," but it was the wrong one. They backed me out and rushed me into the right Operating Room. I was told to cross my arms and they were going to roll me onto my side. They lifted me from the laboring bed to the operating table. It felt like a thousand faces surrounded me. I heard yelling to "hurry up" and different voices asking where my doctor was.

They sounded like voices echoing in a chamber; they were loud, piercing, and terrifying. They were urgent cries for help, and no one was coming.

I heard the instruments being counted and could tell they were being laid out near my belly. I couldn't see past the blue curtain that had been placed across my chest. I heard a nurse ask a man that was standing near my head, "Can *you* do a C-section?"

Oh my God.

The man answered: "…can't anymore, not licensed."

I heard a different, frantic voice: "Where is her OBGYN!?"

Another said, "Her OBGYN says fifteen minutes away." I wanted to die. I didn't know what was going on, but knew *someone* had to do *something*. I just laid there, with tears streaming down my face and pooling in my ears. Time had come to a standstill. No one was doing anything.

Everything was ready, but there was no one there to help, no one there to start the C-section. I quietly said over and over, "Hurry up…hurry up…hurry up…"

I heard a man's voice whisper in my ear, "It's okay, Noelle. I am right here. It will be okay. They are almost here. God is with you. He is here." Almost 35 minutes after being rushed out of my room to the OR, my doctor finally came. She literally ran in and quickly cut me open. She was quiet, asking few questions. As she made the incision, I felt a lot of pressure. She pulled Finley out. The whole room was silent.

I saw out of the corner of my left eye a tiny body being flung to another nurse. The body was grey and had stuff all over it. There was no sound coming from her. They whisked her into a clear incubator, and I closed my eyes. I could hear them, "One—two—three—four…one-two-three-four…" They were using a bag to breathe life into her. I asked, "Is she crying? What is wrong? What is going on with her?"

The man with the sweet voice said, "She's not doing well, Noelle. I am here with you." All of a sudden, the noises and the group of people working on her left the room. The room became quite except for the counting of instruments by my OBGYN. She said nothing to me, but chatted with a staff member about personal business. *Just an average day in the OR?*

I wanted to jump off the OR table and chase after my baby. I didn't want to lay there listening to my OBGYN talk about her life. My life was crumbling in that moment. She finished stitching up my C-section area and the team wheeled me into a small room with even-smaller curtained-off rooms. There was a nurses' area in the middle.

I was shaking violently. I later learned that the medication they gave me on top of the Pitocin caused the excessive shaking. They put me into at heated bag that had heat pumped into it. My body felt like it was convulsing. I wanted to die. I couldn't get my body to calm down and I was scared. I didn't know what was going on. And I didn't know where my Finley was.

I could see my OBGYN and her partner (*wait-both of them?*) in the nurses' station. They were looking at something very intently. I wanted them to come check on me, but they didn't. They were too busy. My family surrounded me—my husband, mom, sister-in-law, and brother. Everyone was crying. The nurses brought in the Baby Book with Finley's feet imprinted. I didn't want to see it. I didn't know what was going on.

A few minutes later, a very abrupt man, who I later found out was the neonatologist that came from another larger hospital, said to me, "It doesn't look good." I lost it. I hated that man. I had no idea who he was, but couldn't believe he told me that. I had already heard that about my dad, three months prior; how could I be hearing that about my daughter? I knew somewhere deep down what that meant. They asked if I wanted to see her.

My mother encouraged me to see her and the transport team brought her in. She was so small, lying in a clear, rolling incubator, looking nothing like I could ever, ever have imagined. Instead of plump and pink, she looked like something out of a science experiment. I couldn't believe that was my Finley. They stayed for one minute and said they had to go, and they did. I couldn't stop crying. I could not comprehend what was happening. *Where were they taking her? What was wrong with her?* Then I came to understand they were taking Finley to a different, larger hospital.

My shaking body finally started calming down and the nurse wheeled me back into the room I had started in. I never made it up to the Mother-Baby Unit. I ended up back on the Labor and Delivery Floor. The nurse told me they thought it would be better. I kept crying, but was so tired. I didn't want to be in one hospital while my baby was somewhere else. They nurse told me I had to stay there in the hospital until the morning, when an ambulance would transport me to the bigger hospital. I told her that they better be there in the morning and when I demanded to know a time, she told me "6 a.m."

My family left and my husband fell asleep.

That night was horrific. I could hear the overheard speakers play a lullaby when a baby was born. Every…single…time. I was in so much pain and felt so alone. I couldn't sleep, though I was exhausted. I finally feel asleep around 4 a.m., only to wake up to my alarm at 6 a.m. The sudden wake-up kicked in a swirl of thoughts. *Was that a nightmare? Did all that really happen?* I quickly realized it was not a nightmare, but real—and that I needed to get on that ambulance.

I called the nurses' station, reminding them that it was 6 a.m. and that the transport team should be picking me up right then. Hours later, they arrived. I was furious. We had kept calling and asking. It seemed like everyone *except* for my nurse would come see me. Finally, the transport team arrived and they moved me onto a smaller stretcher. My husband gathered up all of our belongings to put in the car and follow us to the other hospital where Finley was. As they pushed me out through the Labor and Delivery door, I saw nurses looking at me, almost trying not to stare. I could see them all down the hallway and at the nurses' station. I thanked them, all of the ones I saw, for helping me. They looked shocked. They were unresponsive. I have seen that moment in time over and over in my dreams. The look on the charge nurse's face was so shocked and downcast when I thanked her. She told me, "You're welcome, honey." She was so sweet.

The transport team wheeled me along, turning and weaving through empty hallways. At one point, one of them didn't know how to get back to the ambulance. They were lost. They finally got me to the ambulance, lifted the stretcher, and put me in. I had never been in an ambulance before. They turned out of the hospital and made their way down streets I had known my entire life. It felt surreal. We then pulled up to the other, larger hospital and they opened the doors, taking me out. They wheeled me into the building and many people were staring. They pushed me onto an elevator and down more hallways, into a very ugly part of the hospital. It was so old.

We were met by a nursing team on the anti-partum wing. I was taken from the stretcher and put into a big bed again. The transport team left.

My Daughter

My husband walked in shortly afterward with our belongings. We had so much to talk through. I told him about the ambulance ride and how I wanted to see Finley as soon as possible. My mom arrived, along with my brother and his wife.

In walked both of my OBGYN physicians, adding to my confusion and upset. *So, "leaving for vacation" did not mean she was actually inaccessible?* Because here she was. Here. Too late. I was angry with them. Very little was said between us. They left after a few minutes and said they would be back the next day to check on me.

I asked the nurse if I could go see Finley. I started wondering if I was in the right area of the hospital for women who had already had their babies, because there wasn't a sense of urgency to get me to see Finley. I thought maybe they didn't know I'd had a baby already. Nothing was making sense.

Finally, I was helped out of the bed and put into a wheelchair, which was an excruciating ordeal for me. I had my husband push me to see her. I needed to. He wheeled me down five long hallways to the neo-intensive care unit (NICU) section of the hospital. We had to check in at the front desk.

There was a small waiting room on the left and a small room on the right. The double doors on the right opened and I saw this room for the first time. It was a large area with a lot of hospital baby carts, each with an infant, each with glowing lights and machines. It was so dark in there. I looked for Finley and I saw her. She was a big baby compared to the others, but so small to me. She was lying on her back, arms straight next to her body, tiny hands clenched.

I then noticed her mouth and thought she had a hair lip (cleft palate). I felt like a bad mother for thinking that, but the tube was in her mouth, pressing against her top lip, and I questioned if she had one or not. The nurse told me she didn't, and that it was just the way the tube was positioned.

I couldn't believe she was real. Her face was smooth and fair, like a porcelain doll, and something about her eyebrows and eyes, though not open, seemed so sweet and innocent. She was right there, but I was afraid to touch her. The nurse shared that since she was on a cooling treatment, there was very strict protocol. That protocol included not touching her much and not holding her for 72 hours. I was okay with that because I knew it would help her.

We stayed, staring at her for some time. "Hello, precious daughter. We love you, Finley Elizabeth…" my husband and I said to her. My husband helped me to lift myself out of my wheelchair at one point to see her better. That was nearly impossible for me, but a mother's love knows no bounds. I felt it for the first time…I would do anything for her.

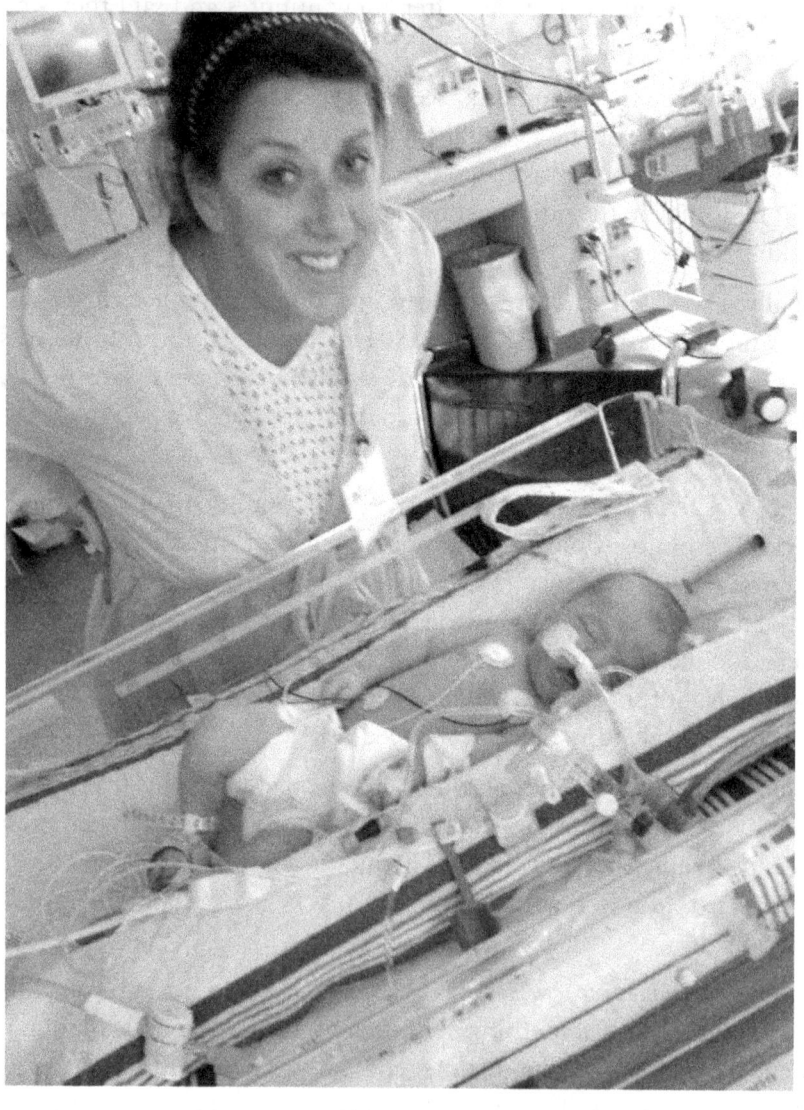

Noelle & Finley, Hospital (2013)

My Daughter

Just This Once, I Must Be Allowed to Turn Back Time

We tried to focus on Finley and her care. Things were so hard to comprehend. We received awful news after a few days—her MRI showed zero brain activity. Finley went far too long without oxygen. An emergency C-section had been clearly called for, but no one performed it until it was too late. Because of this one inexcusable delay, we now faced a daughter that was a shell of a little girl. It appeared that because there was not a physician on property and we waited for our OBGYN to return to perform a C-section, our daughter died.

We as her parents had to picture a child in a way that we never thought we would, as a vegetable. It is such a gross and disgusting word, but that's where my mind went. I tried to hold onto hope, but something in me felt like things were unrelentingly awful. Would she make it? Would they figure out a surgery they could do? Would she wake up and everything be fine? I felt like I was out of my body, floating around her room when we found out her first MRI showed nothing. I couldn't believe it.

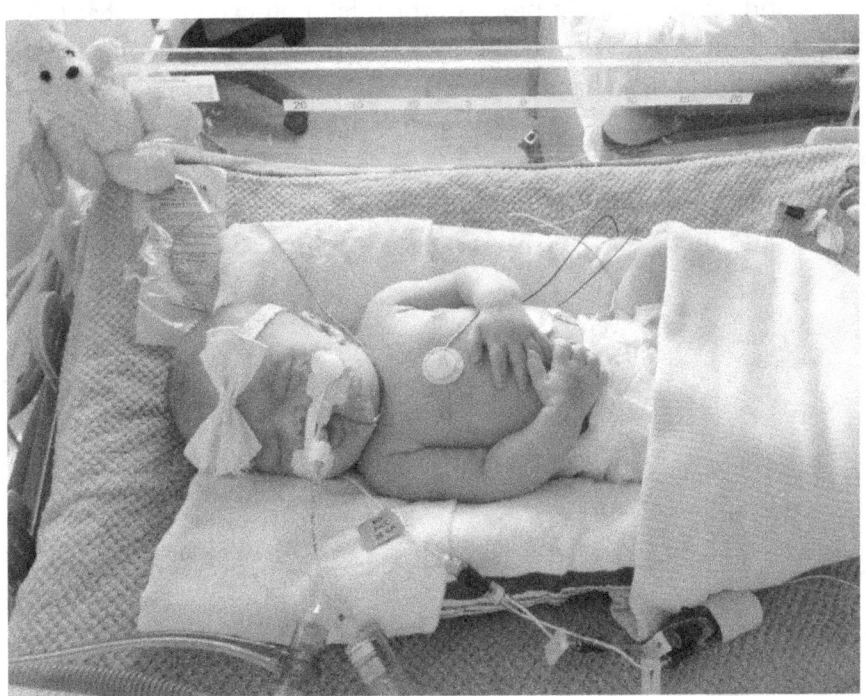

Finley Elizabeth (2013)

In my state of disbelief and denial, I asked if we could take her to a different country. Wasn't there some progressive treatment somewhere, somehow? I had to do something as her mother, since so much of this felt like my fault. I had been the one to choose the hospital; I chose the doctors and this city. Why did I do all of this? Why was I so stubborn? I started tearing into my personhood because I hated myself and all that I had done.

I fervently wished that I could turn back time. I wished so hard, so intently, that it almost felt possible that everything could wind back to before my dad's death, back to my wedding day, back to being happy and still filled with dreams. Just this once, I must be allowed to turn back time!

Over the days and weeks that ensued, I started to lose hope in everything. I couldn't understand why things were happening this way and why Finley wasn't getting better. We went to the hospital every day and every night. We didn't want to miss a moment with her. My husband and I discussed doing three MRIs and, after that, making "the decision" the doctors told us would need to be made. I hated that. It put the weight of the world on my thought process, which felt non-existent at that time. I didn't want to hold the fate of my daughter's life in my hand or head. I wanted the Lord to handle it.

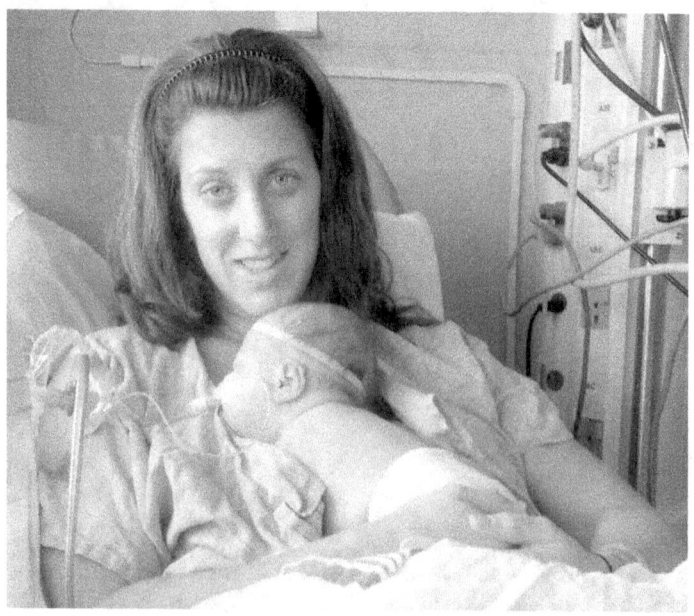

Noelle & Finley, Hospital (2013)

My Daughter

I cried out to God and begged Him, pleading with Him that I would "show the world" if He would heal her. I would "tell of His Glory and that He is real." I needed a miracle and tried to believe in that possibility. I'd heard of people's prayers being answered and felt like I had been a faithful friend of the Lord, so He would help us. He would rescue my sweet little Finley from death's door. He would pull out all the stops.

My husband believed the same thing. His faith was strong, and he prayed over our baby girl. He *knew* she could be healed, and her brain function could come back in one blink of an eye. We both believed what we wanted to believe with all of our hearts. However, after the second MRI, we learned there was no brain activity. The third MRI…NOTHING. Absolutely nothing in her perfectly-shaped beautiful round head that would make her know us or walk, talk, or dance on her own. She wasn't there and I now wasn't either. I wanted to die.

We grieved together once we heard the news. The agony was grueling. The pain palpable. I wanted to leave the pain but didn't know how. I needed to find a place to put it below me and move over it and above it, but life wasn't like that for us.

We almost immediately left the hospital once the team of physicians told us about the last MRI. I wanted to get away from her. I didn't want to bond with her anymore. I was so mad at her or the thought of her not being mine anymore. We drove home and as soon I got out of the car and walked into the house, I saw a sea of faces. People stared at me. I felt like a seething bull in a teeny tiny pen and I needed to get out. It felt like everyone was expecting *something* from me, but I had nothing.

I ran down to the end of our street to the cul-de-sac and stopped, suddenly feeling like a statue that could not move its legs. I sobbed loudly and uncontrollably. Through my tears, I saw a woman walking towards me with a pack of Kleenex. I recognized her as my friendly neighbor who walked her white fluffy dogs. She said four words: "I know that cry." Then she hugged me. Years later, I learned that her 18-year-old son died in a car accident. She truly did know that cry.

My husband and I held each other that night, crying the entire night after the news that she would never know us, never hear her mom and dad say "I love you," never let us hear her sweet little-girl voice, not even once.

The Primal Scream

What is more hard-wired into DNA than **maternal instinct**? Obviously, that is crucial for a complex species (like humans) to survive. When a mom loses her child, it is devastating to her at a cellular level. It is a failure which is felt at the core of her being. She did not ensure that her offspring survived. No matter that she had no part in the current tragedy, her body and psyche will let out a primal scream. There is nothing she can do about that built-in response.

A lot of the primal scream happens within the sound-proof chamber of a mother's heart. No one else hears it. But, sometimes, the primal scream erupts through a mother's raw throat and sends loud, piercing sound waves through every life form within her radius. That volcanic eruption of pure grief happened to me while I was standing by a bay window overlooking a calm, blue lake, shimmering with sunny reflections. The scene through the window was so incongruent with my dark and stormy emotions, I wondered to myself, *how is it possible the sun is shining at all?*

My friends and family were huddled in the NICU lobby and a selected handful of them started to make their way into our lakefront NICU room on the day Finley was supposed to leave us. We gathered in the back corner of Finley's NICU room as the doctors and nurses began making preparations. My husband held her as hospital staff moved about. The doctor came in, the same one that had broken the news to me that there was no chance my baby would recover, and I knew it was almost time. Finley's almost month of living was almost over; I could barely breathe.

The doctor walked over to Finley, where she lay cradled in her father's arms. The doctor looked at me and nodded his head. My husband and I nodded ours. It was time to let her go. The doctor removed the tube from her mouth, and she took her last breath. That was the first time I saw her little blue-grey eyes open. Then she was gone. Up from the center of my gut came the cry, much more intense than I had ever felt before. I knew she was dead, and the pain, the primal scream, erupted.

Suddenly I felt panicked that I didn't know where I belonged. I couldn't stay in that room, but I couldn't leave either. *Where did I belong?* That question has haunted me since. Not belonging anywhere.

My Daughter

We handed Finley over to the two sweetest nurses in the world, Nurse Robin and Nurse Rosie. They promised me they would take care of her. For one final time, I kissed Finley on the head and realized she was cold. That was shocking. I then grabbed my husband and we sobbed our way down the NICU hallway for the last time. We knew those other rooms had babies, but we would no longer be a part of this group. We were now outsiders.

We pushed the elevator button and went down the world's longest elevator ride. I could barely stand. I felt like my body was going to sink into the ground. Outside, my sister had our car waiting for us and the staff put me into the back of the car. My sister drove off and I thought I was going to die. We had plans to go to our friend's house afterwards because the last thing I wanted to do was go home and think. My sister asked if we wanted something to drink and she ran in and got us 7-Eleven Slurpees. I always think of that day when I see Slurpees now.

We ended up at my friend's house where others were waiting to be with us, eat, and drink. I just couldn't function. I wanted to shrivel up as the pain was too much to bear. As I was sitting there, I noticed that across the lake, I could still see the hospital, I could still "see" my daughter. Not long after, I saw a rainbow form directly over the hospital, overarching the very top of the building. I cried and smiled at once. We spent a few hours at their house as I grew more and more anxious to leave—but I didn't know where I wanted to go. The only place I wanted to go was to be with Finley.

We eventually headed home, but the heaviness and strangeness in my house made me feel like a trapped wild animal. All sorts of people were there, and I wanted them to leave. I couldn't think straight. I went upstairs and hid in my room.

It's hard for others to understand what not knowing where you belong feels like, but try with me for a moment. Picture this: Your brain is a blurry mess, and nothing aligns. Your eyes can barely stay open, but closing them is worse. You have a headache from crying and images of your child flash through your mind, sometimes when they were alive, other times when they were dying or were there, lifeless. You cannot think straight, you cannot see straight, you don't care about food, nor who is coming or who is going. Nothing matters except that you want your child back. The longing, the ache, throbs mercilessly.

Nothing functions as it should. To take a shower is a major feat because it seems futile when your child is dead. To eat or brush your teeth doesn't really cross your mind because you can't stop crying long enough to do either one of those things. Driving a car even a mile to the store is completely out of the question. You live with a constant lump in your throat, one that you try to push down just to talk. Tears pour out constantly and breathing feels hard at times. People ask questions but you can't hear them and can't figure out words to make a sentence for an answer. You don't want anyone around, yet you certainly don't want to be alone.

That is what the early hours and days of grief look like. That is what my days looked like. As I sat upstairs on that first day, I knew I should not look into Finley's freshly painted and adorably decorated room, but I did. There were the baby bottles and soft pink blankets that would never be picked up to soothe her. For her, for myself...I felt so cheated.

My milk was coming in so I had a constant reminder of a baby I would never feed. I had to pump, and the physical pain was almost unbearable. Nature took its course, but humans failed me. I was so angry and alone. My husband had shut down. No one was there in a way that helped me—I certainly didn't care about eating the endless food that people brought over.

Some people apparently thought if they acted "normal," we could all feel okay again. No, I did not want to be engaged in conversation about where to go see pretty fall leaves in a few weeks. There was no such thing as tomorrow, much less, October.

But there was a bright spot in all of this mess. I remember the day after Finley died, a handful of my friends came over and we went up to my room, away from all the other people crowding my small townhome. We sat on my bed and ate candy. That made me happy. They just sat with me, and tears poured almost the entire time. They were scared, I could tell, but they were there with me and for me. That is what it's all about. Showing up even when you are scared and feel helpless to help. As my friend, Lane Alexander, always said. "It's such uncharted territory for so many people. They don't want to do it wrong, so they just sometimes don't do it."

That day, true friends and candy got me through.

CHAPTER 5

My Husband

My dear friend booked a cruise for my husband and me so we could leave very soon after Finley died. We sailed away from shore, but our pain went with us. It was a strange, surreal, and very sad time. I was glad to be away from everyone, but I couldn't get my head to clear.

Sitting at a large round table one evening for dinner, other cruise guests were trying to be social and talk with us. I couldn't find words to speak and didn't want to tell them what had just happened. I went in and out of being present, churning with pain and awkwardness, and being a million miles away, zoned out and not even hearing what other guests were saying to me. It felt like a nightmare.

To think the world was just going on, yet my daughter had just died, was an impossible reality to face. I could not dredge up one single thought that gave me comfort. Well, there was one, and I became fixated on it. Lying in bed each night, I begged my husband for another child. I wanted one so desperately. I needed to know I would be a mom again and that my life would have meaning. He was too upset and afraid to agree, which made me more upset. How could he not give me the one thing I needed? How could he rob me of the only thing I ever wanted in my life? The frustration and hopelessness were mounting, and I was scared.

We returned from our 3-night cruise and arrived back at our home. Reality seemed inescapable there and I couldn't stop crying. Our first night back, he wasn't talking to me or showing any emotion. I was hurting and wanted him to hurt too or at least show me he was hurting. I was desperate for empathy, sympathy, anything. We got into a huge fight because I felt like he was shutting down and he went downstairs. I was so angry with him and didn't bother to check to see where he went. I woke up three hours later to pump milk as the pain was almost unbearable. I cried so hard I could barely see to use the breast pump. I was so angry! *Why am I pumping when there is no baby to give this to!!* I finally laid down and fell asleep, only to wake up with a flash of horror and fear, hoping it was a nightmare. It wasn't. I started to cry.

My husband was scheduled to go back to work that day, so when I came downstairs and didn't see him, I assumed he had already left for work. I tried calling him, but he did not answer. I tried texting and no response. I called again and left a voice mail. The morning went on and I heard nothing. I tried time after time, but he wouldn't get back to me. I was getting more and more upset.

I had a Women's Ministry event at church, which my mom (who was staying in our home at the time) urged me to attend. I couldn't think clearly for myself, so I planned my day around it. Maybe she was right that I should go. I got dressed and left in the early afternoon to head for the church. I could barely keep my eyes open, could not focus on what was being said, and could barely talk to the women around me. I didn't belong there—or anywhere. I didn't want to be home; I didn't want to be at church. I didn't want to be in my car, and I didn't want to be outside. Finally, the event was over and I headed home, consumed with worry and anger that I had not once heard from my husband all day.

When I arrived home, I didn't see my husband's car outside. *Hmm… maybe he went to Walmart.* When I walked in, my mother was sitting in the guest room watching TV. I yelled, "Mom! Have you seen him?"

She said, "He was coming and going, but I didn't know what he was doing." I got mad.

"How could you not know what he was doing? Did you ask him why he wasn't at work?" I ran upstairs and there was my explanation.

There was a pile of clothes, cards, and other items stacked up on my bed. My mind was racing. I turned to my right to see our closet was half-emptied. I realized that the pile of clothes were items I had given him as gifts and the cards were special cards from holidays and special moments. I realized that half the closet was empty because he must have taken his clothes. It was at that moment, I couldn't breathe.

Catching my breath, I started screaming. I felt an even more intense pain then when Finley had died, probably because rage was now coursing through me. There was a large picture frame propped up against my wall with the glass next to it. I grabbed the glass and threw it across the room. I immediately felt a sharp pain in my hand. Blood was gushing from it, dripping all over the beige carpet. I grabbed a towel and yelled to my mom, "Let's go!"

I knew I had done something stupid and that I needed to get to the Emergency Room. I had picked up that piece of glass because I was so devastated that I didn't know what to do with my emotions. I was furious, angry, outraged. My mind couldn't wrap around the fact that my husband had betrayed me, that he came into our home while I was gone and took all of his possessions. The cowardly and cruel man *I was married to* had simply abandoned me.

I was having a nervous breakdown.

At the local hospital ER, my brother arrived and told me he had finally gotten hold of my husband. He was going to come to the hospital. I felt shame and embarrassment because I didn't want him to see me that way, but on the flipside, relief because he was my best friend and husband. However, relief is not what he provided. Instead, he came into my ER room, berating me and asking what happened. "What did you do to yourself? Why did you do that? What is wrong with you?"

I started crying even harder. He said a few more words and stood up. He wanted to leave. So, there I sat, my hand and clothes covered in blood, and my husband starting to walk out. The emergency room double doors pushed open and he walked through them. A shrill scream came up and out from my body, much like when Finley had died. "NO! Please don't go!" But he kept walking and I chased after him. I yelled to him, but I finally stopped because he got in his car. I sobbed in the dark hospital parking lot, while he got into our old-run-down Volkswagen and pulled away. My heart was done. My body was done. I couldn't go on anymore.

Someone brought me back inside and I cried for hours. My hand was injured much more severely than I could have imagined from one grab and sling of glass. They had to stitch me up 19 times to stop the bleeding. Thank God my mother was there with me at the hospital. She was an angel, comforting me as best she could.

Eventually, we were able to leave and she drove me back home. Much more distressing than the injury was my state of shock. I was in such a haze. I couldn't even process what my husband—the person imprinted in my mind as my long-time best friend, lover, prayer partner, father of my child—had done that day. He had moved out and ignored my calls. Then he came to the hospital to say mean things to me. Then he drove away. My heart was broken.

The next few days were brutal. I tried over and over to reach my husband, but he wouldn't respond. After the day that Finley died, I never heard from anyone in his family. No one checked on me or asked how I was doing except for one of his aunts. I was so thankful for her.

I said that my heart was broken, but I was to learn that shattering has many layers. Over the next days and weeks, my heart broke piece by piece, little by little.

Abandonment

Divorce after infant loss is horrific. My husband leaving me was in many ways worse than my baby dying. Now, I felt so abandoned, alone, angry, frustrated because of someone's untimely and heartless choice. The pain felt unbearable, truly. I couldn't get him to respond or want to help me. I had to deal with a 10-ton savage gorilla alone. The 10-ton burden was not only huge but complex, including my little angel's death, the issues with the hospital, and the terrible fact that the OBGYNs had left me and Finley, resulting in tragic consequences. I also carried the emptiness of no longer having an identity as a wife or mother. I felt like nothing, but had to be everything.

The silence and emptiness in my soul scared me. My thoughts scared me. Nothing anyone said mattered or helped. I wanted my husband back. I wanted my life back.

I Thought We Were Best Friends

We met years before getting married and were dear friends, telling each other just about everything. We were more friends than lovers, but that was okay with me. He was a wonderful man, with a lot to learn, but an open heart.

After my dad's death in 2013, my husband and I struggled to find our footing. Deciding where to live and where would be best for my mom became the largest source of contention. His family sided with him, thinking my mother would do well in their hometown. I disagreed.

My Husband

They were mad. For the first time in my life, I remember thinking people were truly stubborn. They didn't consider my mom's feelings and how she would do in a new state with new people. She lost her partner, lover, and other half. Must everything familiar to her being ripped away as well? I pushed back and fought against their "decision." They thought I was "rebellious" and not appropriately submissive. Boy, they didn't know me. I have always fought for the rights of others, especially the helpless and in this instance, the helpless was my mother.

After pushing back, my family, with almost zero concurrence, decided to move our mother back to our home state. She seemed peaceful about that. We moved her out of the home she had lived in with my father. We threw away his clothes, his belongings—so many memories gone in a dumpster. It hurt. It was so hard. We finally were able to pack up her house and move all of her belongings down to our home state, a place I hadn't lived in for ten years.

My husband chose to stay with his parents while I moved my mother into our new house. I did this while 6 months pregnant with help from my family. He never came to help. This started building the hard spot in my heart towards him and others. I felt like I had no choice other than to move our things, but with no help. Reflecting on that time, I have no idea how I did all that work, in the hot heat, being 6 months pregnant; no man in site except my brother and my sister's friends. No husband there to help his hurting wife.

The months leading up to Finley's birth and death were stressful and lonely. Not only was my husband not on board to support me, I missed my dad terribly. He was my life-long best friend. Losing him (five months before losing Finley) was the first time I knew grief. I was sad that such a wonderful man was gone from our family, and I especially grieved over my own loss of his rock-solid love and support I had always leaned into. He kept me going many times in business, life, relationships. He was my main man and when he died, I felt so lost. I became a caregiver to my incredible mom—somehow finding the energy to be a comforting companion, helper, and encourager—all the while pregnant, tired, and lonely. Finley became my hope for new joys and new life.

Finally, after three months of living in my home state and getting my mother settled, my husband reluctantly moved to be with me. I don't know what came over me, but I truly was excited for him to come be with me. I think I pushed down that hard part in my heart because I craved someone that wanted to be with me and help me. I was tired of doing everything alone. I picked him up from the airport and we met like long-lost lovers seeing each other after a war.

We were very happy to be with each other again. Deep down, however, I still had the bitterness of not being supported and helped after my dad's death. He had left me to fend for myself.

He struggled to find a job, partially because of his attitude and unwillingness; mostly because of his work history being limited to military.

I found it so hard to believe that this person who had felt like a true friend for so long did not rise to the occasion when I really needed his support. Like the stock market, trends don't lie, and his pattern was to avoid situations and people when the going got tough. Unlike myself, who digs in to a fault, pushing the point to no end, he did not want to work on fixing our situation, our relationship, our life. My dreams were shattering in front of me. It was much worse than I could have ever imagined.

In July, when he went with me to the one and only prenatal appointment in Florida, I felt connected, but still bitter. I felt happy he was there, but sad that he had missed all of the prior ones. It is nothing short of miraculous to see your baby's image through an ultrasound and I could not imagine why that baby's father would not be doing whatever it took to be there to witness that. And I needed him. I didn't want to do all of this by myself, even though I had done just that.

When Finley was first born, but in peril, he was great. We were connected, communicating, crying together, and talking. He was the strong one in many ways. We would pray on the way to the hospital every morning and talk about her plan of care for the day. We were both very open and honest in the days after her birth. We would hold each other, help each other, and encourage each other. I was a wreck and he would remind me about "God's goodness." He assured me many times that God was not going to forsake us. I was thankful for this strength I had seen a handful of times, although it was missing after my dad's death.

Something weighed him down and weakened him after my dad died. I don't know if it was his parents, but that's what I suspected. They weren't like my family. We talked openly about things and whether right or wrong at times, we dealt with things head on. His family swept things under the rug and always put on the face of "everything is fine." They never reached out to me after my dad passed away, never checked on their only grandchild who was growing in my womb, nor did they encourage my husband to work things out with me. They coddled him and made him feel his decision to live apart from me was the right one. I disagreed and despised them because of this.

When they showed up at the hospital after Finley's birth, I hated seeing their faces. They had stopped treated me as a family member who they really cared about and my bitter self was in no mood to see them. But I was trapped in that little hospital room, forced to see and hear their apparent distress.

At that point, we all knew that Finley's delivery had been problematic and that she was under intensive care. I felt like they blamed me for everything and that the accident was my fault for being so "rebellious." If I had gone to their hometown hospital, none of this would have happened. Their streaming tears and sad faces made me feel awful, like eyes burning into my skull. I felt ashamed. On top of all of my turmoil, they were there to pile on more shame.

This was all my fault and they knew it. If only I had been a submissive and compliant wife, then Finley would have been cared for and alive; instead, she was left in the care of two physicians who were so negligent that she died. My choice of doctors and hospital was the reason for Finley not being able to come into this world in the timely manner she should have.

Even when not around his family, my husband stayed in his own thoughts, I guess dealing with his own pain in whatever way he could. As Finley's father, one would assume that he would be most empathetic to me, but he was choosing to deal with his grief much differently than I was.

He filed for divorce, and walked away. I never again heard from him or his family.

When he left, I was even more desperate for help than the day Finley died. My waning hope that he would come through once he'd had time to recover was now taken away with one final slam of that door. I started to think I wasn't going to make it.

More Than "I'm Sorry"

CHAPTER 6

The Outsider

It was in the moment she died that I became the outsider, but in some way an insider to a new group—a club no one wants to belong to. I was pushed out by mostly my own sadness, away from people, especially my friends with little kids. I couldn't stand the site of a small baby as it literally made me feel physically sick. My pain was so heavy that seeing another baby only made me feel hurt and so unfairly robbed.

Finley's Gravesite

I began to learn that loss finds a special place tucked inside your heart…and that it never goes away. There are outings with friends, small vacations with family, days filled with meetings, workout sessions and long walks—none of these things can erase the fact that a sweet, innocent child is no longer with us. No activity, no conversation, no distraction wipes away the painful memory that my only daughter died in front of me.

The first year after she died, 2013, was such a blur. The haze, the fog, the overarching feeling that *this was not my life* is what consumed my every day. I had to figure out how to just get through each minute, then an hour, and eventually each day. I found myself wandering, where nothing made me feel better, but just being made me feel worse.

Looking back, I realize that many days I was trying to outrun the pain. I found myself frequently shopping, ordering takeout instead of cooking or going to a restaurant, and running up credit cards without much thought. I found myself becoming something I never thought I would—physically as well as emotionally unhealthy. Instead of feeling fulfilled or relieved by my activities, I walked around feeling more and more disoriented.

New Territory for Yes and No

I fell into trying too hard to please other people. There were times when people invited me to things and although I was appreciative, I should have said, "no." Just a few months after Finley's death, I was invited to a one-year-old's birthday party. I felt awful in every respect and my brain was in such a cloud of grief, I wasn't thinking straight. Of course, I should have politely declined the invitation, but I said *okay*. The mom was one of my closest friends and I didn't want to upset her.

I made the wrong choice. I arrived in the suburban neighborhood shaking, then parked my car and wiped away wet tears streaming down my cheeks. I quickly placed sunglasses on my face to hide the pain I didn't want anyone there to see. I felt dumb.

I finally got the courage to walk into the party and the room seemed to fall out underneath me. Talk about feeling like an outsider. No one knew what to do in that first minute and their expressions of confusion, sadness, pity, and even fear…all added up to the most awkward entrance anyone ever made in the history of the world.

I slowly walked towards everyone, while sounds of jubilant children running around filled the background. I could see smiles turn into horizontal stretched lines and eyes begin to drift down. I stood there like a statue. Some people came over to give me a hug. I squeezed back lightly, for fear of losing too much control and then not being able to recover. I was holding myself together, piece by piece, moment by moment.

My mind was screaming at me to turn around and leave, but my other inner voice fought that plan because I certainly did not want to be back at home, either. There was no place I *wanted* to be. I felt angry with myself for not being able to cheer up a bit for the sake of these dear friends. We had a rich history, the stuff that makes up the best stories, stories to be told again and again on long nights of shared drinks and laughter. These were my people.

I didn't know how to fit in anymore. I was glad they invited me, but I was discovering something: it was up to them to invite and up to me to decide.

Protecting one's emotions, feelings, and sanity itself is critical in the early stage after loss. Grief pours on a heaviness that can be scary and must be managed. It is not always best to throw oneself into a situation to test the waters early on, as this can set off emotions that have yet to be tamed. A grieving mom should never have an expectation of how long it will take for her to feel any relief. There is no calendar to follow, only paying attention to her own state of mind and emotions.

It is up to the grieving mother to decide if she is in a place to attend a party, come over for coffee, attend church services, or even talk on the phone. One mom shared: "I literally could not talk on the phone for many months. At first, I had a friend come over and make calls for me as I sat at my desk at home and determined who needed to be called about what. I will never forget how much that helped me."

I Did Not Sign Up for This

I so desperately wanted to feel like myself again. Like a toddler throwing a tantrum, I fought against what I was feeling. I did not want this to be me, certainly not the new me. The one emotion that scared me the first year after losing my daughter was anger. I was always a passionate, assertive person in many ways, but the anger and rage simmering inside me was unrecognizable. I felt outrage about the way that she died, the negligence, about waking up every day now to this new life that I did not sign up for. I was angry about my husband leaving and so many other things—I felt a little afraid of the raging bull inside myself. Anger is essentially what drove me into getting counseling. I was afraid that I would not only emotionally hurt others, but I knew I was hurting myself.

Starting with that moment that Finley died, I knew that I needed help, but I couldn't figure out what would help me. It was when I left the hospital that I felt and saw the huge gap between the hospital and being home, living my life. I needed help but couldn't find the place to get it.

Days went on and on. I didn't know where to go or who was going to help. My husband wasn't around and my family did not understand the level of my distress and pain. How could they. I felt like I needed professional help.

There were many groups and articles online, but there was very little if anything that was comprehensive in nature. I decided to reach out to a local place that others had said could help me. It was a grief center. With enormous effort, I was able to gather myself for a minute and stop crying. I picked up the phone to call and they answered. I found out they are a grief program that helps children who experience grief, along with adults, but I would have had to have a child in order to attend their groups and be a part of their program. Just when I thought I couldn't take one more punch in the gut, there it was. Adding insult to injury, they said that since I didn't have a (living) child, they couldn't help me. *This is the way my life is going to go now? I did not sign up for this!*

What's To Be Done with Mothers Like Me?

I was mad, but not so much at them, because I knew they were doing good things, but mad at this notion that no one knows what to do with mothers like me who lose their child. I knew I was not the only mother who had suffered this horrible kind of loss. It felt like the whole world was ignoring me (and the other grieving mothers). Professional help is so readily available for all kinds of mental and emotional hardships, from anxiety to sex addiction, but no one could come up with any appropriate resource for me.

Getting into counseling a few weeks after she died was hard. I did not know where to go. I did not even understand how it would work or if it could actually help. I reached out to some family and they located a husband and wife that did counseling. I was apprehensive, but I was so desperate that I didn't care that the counselor was not a grieving-mother specialist and was a male, though I did wonder if he could possibly understand my trauma.

The counseling practice was in a really beautiful part of town and I remember feeling peaceful when I would start seeing those streets lined with large oak trees, original 1920s buildings, and then his office in an upstairs space with a large, picture window. I could see the large oaks from the comfy couch; sometimes I would lean into their strength. It was in that room that I felt like my healing started.

With kindness and patience, I was guided to walk through the most painful moments since my daughter died, especially my husband walking out. This is a part of my life that hurts to even write. He is and always will be Finley's dad and I don't regret loving him for his many good qualities. But he chose a different way to grieve and try to heal from our loss. Instead of walking through the grief and dealing with it, he ran away. It was in counseling that I had to painfully deal with the fact that the very person I needed more than anyone left me. I hoped that through counseling I could understand why he suddenly packed up his things when I wasn't home and left me to deal with my daughter's death alone. That came scary-close to putting me over the edge.

The grueling silent agony of being so alone was almost deafening. The quiet in the silence was almost unbearable. That is why going to counseling and using my voice to put words to feelings practically saved my life. Inside I was feeling so much, but I had to get it out. I had to talk to someone that could assure me that I could make it even if it meant doing it without my husband.

As it turned out, this counselor and his wife saved my life. I would count down the days and hours until my next appointment. He became my lifeline for living because some days, just knowing I would get to go there kept me sane. His wife eventually did hypnotherapy on me, which was an incredibly powerful tool, as it made me safely address the underlying Post Traumatic Stress Disorder I had because of the way Finley died. Watching your child die is not natural. As I said, it is horrifying to every strand of DNA in every cell in a mother's soul.

For years, I fought against my identity. Often, a woman's identity is wrapped up in being a wife and/or a mother, but I did not have either. I was like a puzzle piece in the wrong set of a picture puzzle. Now an outsider, I did not fit.

Like a football player pressing against defensive line training pads, I felt myself pressing against this new identity that I was given, one that I did not sign up for. To reassemble my old "normal" life, I twisted and turned things to try to make them fit, but it wasn't working.

The years starting ticking by and the pain lessened some, but I ached with desire for a new life, a new family. I dated men, hoping to meet someone that could dream with me and want to create the life I always wanted. It was not easy walking into a date with a new man, thinking about all the things I had going on inside of me. I worked my face into one resembling a calm, smiling human, hoping it would mask all the churning emotions and tragic characters inside me that I was sure no sane person would want to meet on a first date.

Not only was I still so, so sad about losing my child and my husband, I had a large amount of shame and guilt piled on. All the *should-haves* and *if-onlys* weighed on my mind. *Why would a new man like me at all once he finds out? Surely he will assume that my husband left because there is something wrong with me?*

I began to get more and more discouraged in my dating endeavors. I decided to not date for a while and just focus on myself. I needed to find new ways to fit in, to not always feel like an outsider. I needed to create a new life where I felt like I belonged.

Whispers of the Heart

My first big "me" thing was deciding to learn guitar, so I got in my car and drove to our local guitar store. I was a fish out of water as I had never played before, but I had the sense that I was following my own heart, that this was *me listening to the new me*. I walked in and asked if they had anyone that taught guitar lessons. They directed me around the corner and as I approached the glass covered counter, I saw a man with a long grey beard and covered in tattoos. I assumed that music was this guy's life. We talked and agreed upon a time for my first lesson. I left the store without buying a guitar...I just had a feeling one would show up for me.

I asked around and found a friend who had a guitar that they were no longer using or wanted...score! I had found not only a guitar, but someone to teach me. I was so proud of myself for both of these things. It felt like a big deal.

Leading up to my first lesson, I was excited and a little scared. I had no idea how this was going to go. I would sit and strum on my guitar at night, but the resulting sounds were atrocious. My first lesson day came and we sat down in two chairs facing each other. My hands felt like large bear paws trying to tip-toe across the neck of the guitar. My fingers were stiff and unfamiliar with how to strum. The lesson finally ended after what seemed like an eternity, but I came out full of joy. I learned one chord! I was very proud of myself.

Noelle learns guitar, Maitland, FL (2013)

Another idea kept whispering to me—painting. I had painted a lot back before I was married, but hadn't picked up a brush in a long time. I went to our local hobby store and purchased a pack full of small paints, a package of assorted paint brushes, and a large canvas. I was set. I loved painting on my back porch. Being outside, sitting on the cement, painting was my new favorite thing. I would put on my favorite songs and just paint. I never knew what I was painting, nor did I have an agenda. I just wanted to experience free-flow creativity.

I also re-connected with another love—working out. As a college athlete, working out was always a part of my daily routine. It felt so right to turn my attention again to my body's strength, flexibility, and stamina. I had always felt comfortable in a gym setting, but this time was different. I had gained a lot of weight from overeating and not doing anything, plus I had a hard time being around people the first few months. I found it especially difficult to walk back into places where the last time I was there, I was pregnant. *What if someone remembers me and asks how my baby is doing?!* It took everything inside of me to walk into the gym.

Eventually I found a morning Zumba dance class that I could go to. I would stand in the very back in case I would cry, hoping no one would see me. I went every other day and loved how I was starting to feel outside. I was waiting for my insides to catch up.

I started to build my confidence back again and found myself moving towards the front. Both my body and mind were improving—dancing was changing my life. Being active and moving again started to make me feel a little more like me. It gave me an outlet and gave me a space for my anxiety and depression to be released.

I have enjoyed taking classes—bootcamp classes, dance classes, combat classes, step classes, yoga, Pilates classes and more. It also felt great to get back into weight training.

I found a night dance class for the "more fit" crowd and attended every class I could. My dance teacher Alaina and other dance mates became new friends. With my new community of fellow dance enthusiasts, I did not feel like an outsider at all. It was amazing.

Noelle, Ritmokru Dance, Orlando, FL (2017)

Dancing, guitar, and painting were helping me to discover/rediscover myself, but some of the main part of me figuring out who I was again would require me doing some of the hard work. The mental health component of me really needed help. I struggled with learning how to deal with so much. As I continued to attend counseling, my counselor said, "You know, sometimes self-care means not really doing anything at all." I didn't understand. "For you, you like to be busy and go and do, but maybe you should consider just 'being.'" The more I thought about it, I knew this was true. My initial and natural inclination is to scurry about, finding things to do, people to talk to, friends to find that could help me "solve" my problems, but what I was beginning to understand is that healing and purpose must be found within myself.

I was learning that it was in the quiet times, the peaceful times, that I could cry, I could process, I could cry out to God for understanding.

I was learning a new rhythm of life—a combination of trying new things with learning to just be still and okay with the real me. It was not easy.

Sometimes the silence after loss is maddening. Over the years, there were times when I wouldn't want to be alone with my thoughts, but I needed to be. There were spans of time where the pain was so deep and vast that I didn't want to deal with any of it. However, the one thing that has transformed by life—from 2013 until today—is that I have pivoted my thinking, my plans, my expectations.

You see, my life was not going how I planned— being a mother, a wife, an entrepreneur. I long dreamt of taking my children to the park and dropping them off at school. Every time I went to a Chic-Fil-A, I pictured watching my children frolic in the play space. I imagined how my whole little family would dress for church on Sunday. I wanted it all—the children, the husband, the snuggly nights watching movies together, yet that all changed. And THAT is what I fought against.

I have learned over the years that in order to find true peace that I have had to pivot from what I thought my life was supposed to look like into something much different, but very uniquely and purposefully mine. To stop being an outsider in my own life, I have put down my weapons of anger, bitterness, frustration, and entitlement to embrace living a life that is designed for me. I have seen God work in amazing ways. I wouldn't have signed up for this, but I know He has used my pain for His purpose. God has used my pain to help other mothers overcome the greatest tragedy on this earth.

The Finley Project Moms Support Group, Maitland, FL (2021)

The Finey Project Moms, Orlando, FL (2020)

The Finley Project Moms, Sanford, FL (2019)

I now find peace knowing that I am okay with myself. I am okay to be alone with just me, I am okay to sit in silence, I am okay even if my deck of cards includes being single and a mother of one angel baby.

I chose to honor my daughter by being the best mother to her I could be. I want her legacy of helping others live again to always be remembered.

More Than "I'm Sorry"

CHAPTER 7

A Map of Hope for the Lost

A person going through this kind of loss needs a compass, a roadmap, and, in that metaphor, some porters alongside to help carry the burdens that are part of any difficult life journey. For a grieving mother, the burdens are just too heavy for her to carry alone, no matter how strong, resilient, and capable she's been in life before this loss. Don't expect otherwise.

The one-on-one counseling was helping me to stay sane, but I could tell I needed much more in the way of support to not feel so awfully alone. Barely able to think and after being turned down by the one grief center, I started reaching out to see if there were other support groups for infant loss. One of the only the only ones I found seemed like it was in connection to the hospital, so I didn't want anything to do with it. I found "GriefShare," a 13-week support group and that saved my life. Two of the leaders, Dale and Elaine Coulter, are the reason I am able to write this today. They were the reason I made it.

Elaine Coulter & Noelle Moore, New Smyrna Beach, FL (2019)

When I started to heal with help from both the support group and counseling, I revisited my feelings of anger and frustration that had overwhelmed me before I found the support I so desperately and urgently required. *Who helps people like me? A mom whose baby was killed or a mom who experiences an infant dying?* It was this question that propelled me to dig, research, and eventually develop the nation's only specialized holistic program: The Finley Project.

Finding helpful support can start with the team at the hospital; but after that, family, friends and others *must step up to help*. A family member's help can look like them finding a good support group for the mom to try—the friend or family member does not have to have the answers, just the commitment to help—as I cover in-depth in my trainings, The Finley Project Model® and my Care Guide for those who want the step-by-step coaching on what a grieving mother *really* needs and how to get those needs met.

No one is well-equipped to handle the loss of a child. Other losses such as losing a grandparent or parent at least seem like a natural endpoint on the circle of life. Jillian A. Carpenter, M.S.W., who is an Assistant Professor in Teaching at the Office of Field Education, School of Social Work, with Virginia Commonwealth University, lost her daughter Logan in 2017. She says that "an out-of-order death" doesn't rationally make sense and that the isolation a mother feels is incredibly intense and unnatural.

As I worked on developing ways to help—really help—grieving mothers in what was formulating into a 7-Step Holistic Program, In one of my conversations with Jillian, she shared, "Trauma causes a fight, flight or freeze response," she said, "and that's why it's imperative for people to step in to help."

You are a person caring enough to read about how to help a grieving mom, and my deepest hope is that I can help more mothers through people like you. Let's cover some pitfalls to avoid and some really helpful actions you will be able to take to make a difference.

Understanding That It's Not About You

This is a hard one—harsh, really, but when helping someone walk the journey of grief, you've got to remember, "It's not about me."

Why does this matter? There are common occurrences that happen when people try to help a hurting person and don't get the response they expected. They get offended and then they stop reaching out. Truly, the best offer of support is like a gift given freely with no need for anything in return. Whatever is going on with the mother, don't take it personally.

> "A well-meaning person needs to know the mom may not yet be ready to receive in-person words of sympathy or a hug. Please don't take it personally. It's like having a bad sunburn ... and she needs space to heal."
>
> Noelle Moore, a mom who's been there

In 2018, our Program was supporting a mother who shared about a time she was invited to a 2-year-old boy's birthday. This mother had just lost her 18-month-old son. As a kind and friendly person in the not-so-distant past, the mother would attend celebrations and get-togethers of any kind. Because of the timing and her immeasurable grief, this event was different.

Her stomach clenched into knots at the thought of pulling onto a street lined with cars and walking into a house filled with parents and boisterous children. She imagined herself having to face her dead son's former playmate, the happy birthday boy, the child she now secretly despised. Yes, this is what grief does. Compounding the pain, this sweet mother felt guilty for her resentment towards this little boy—it wasn't his fault that her son had died in a drowning accident. It wasn't his fault she may never be able to have more children, or that her husband is distant. So, this mother did the only thing she could do—she decided not to go.

She waited until the morning of the party in hopes that she would somehow feel differently and be fine to go. Anxiously and nervously, she sent a text to the boy's mom that said she "was so sorry, but [she] couldn't come."

She did what she needed to do, only to get the response that happens too often: "Well, that's strange. I thought you said you are going to come by. It will be good for you, don't you think? To get out of the house and see everyone?"

Can you see how that selfish reply was packed with guilt and other shaming overtones of pressure? Dear Birthday Boy's Mom: It's not about you.

"No Thanks" Usually Means "Not Yet"

Like the face of a coin, the face of grief does become less sharply defined; its sharp edges wear a little smoother over time.

When someone's offer of what THEY think would be supportive is declined, it is a mistake for them to just back off and neglect to try again later. Even if they've reached out several times, they should not give up because the grieving person isn't responding fast enough in the time frame they expect.

It's important to remember that a grieving person is often barely hanging on and all they can do to make it through a few minutes without crying is just to make it through. In the instances where someone doesn't text back or return a phone call, guess what can be done? REACH OUT again. Don't quit. The hurting person sees the call, the text, the card—and it may be all that is keeping them alive for that day.

No one can say when the time is "right." If a friend continues to check in, offers to help, or extends an invitation, one day it will be at just the perfect time.

"Grief is not linear. It's not a slow progression forward toward healing, it's a zigzag, a terrible back-and-forth from devastated to okay until finally there are more okay patches and fewer devastated ones. The mind can't handle emotions like grief and terror for any sustained period of time, so it takes some downtime." – Lisa Unger, author, *Beautiful Lies*

When a loss first happens, most people are surrounded by a handful of supportive people, whether it's friends, family, hospital staff, church members, gym partners, or neighbors. Some people have a larger community—I've seen a mother who received calls and cards from hundreds of people. However, over time, the support always dwindles. People go back to work, return their attention to their own families, start prepping for holidays, planning birthdays and carrying on life as normal or very nearly normal. Sadly, just when they pull away may be when the grieving person most needs to connect. Their shock is wearing off and their fog is lifting. They are just "starting to think," but don't know what resources there are and need help.

This is the time, usually after six months, to stick by the grieving person because the reality is really setting in. "Seventy-eight percent of participants indicated that over time, the type of support they needed changed. Reasons for this changing need, selected from a priority list with an additional option for open text ('other' option), included relying more on themselves (36%), needing more formal professional one-on-one support (33%), and still needing support, but not as often as before (32%). Thirty-one percent indicated that they relied more on family and friends for support over time. When asked about whether or not they were able to get the support they needed over time, 23% of total participants responded 'yes, definitely'." That small percentage shows that people really do need help over time and often feel forgotten as months pass. https://bmcpregnancychildbirth.biomedcentral.com/articles/10.1186/s12884-019-2270-2

Deep Empathy

Stepping into someone's pain is incredibly difficult, but it's an honorable thing. I did this with the Johnson family. Wearing a brave smile and a look that conveys deepening pain, I met my fellow grieving mother Chelsea Johnson, mother to angel baby Christopher Johnson, in December 2014. She was that person whom you meet and the chord that connects pulls so strongly that you immediately feel a sense of unity. Chelsea was one of the first mothers I helped after starting The Finley Project. She was a mother that desperately needed guidance after her son Christopher died.

Chelsea Johnson & Noelle Moore, Orlando, FL (2020)

More Than "I'm Sorry"

Here's her story: Chelsea and her husband were expecting twins. Chelsea had always prayed for twins and her persistent prayers were answered. She and her husband would be having a boy and a girl. However, when the babies were born, they realized that their daughter Calay had some abnormalities, while their son Christopher displayed all healthy behaviors and abilities. Calay was different. She was diagnosed with Triple X syndrome, a genetic disorder with no cure. Her parents dealt with this head-on, embracing her and loving her just as they did their sweet Christopher. Life was good in the Johnson household for many months and time ticked by, the babies grew stronger/healthier and Calay seemed to be doing great, but everything changed.

One winter afternoon, the twins were put down for their usual nap. They fell fast asleep and their parents went about their business. After an hour or so, their dad came to check on them to wake them up from their nap. It was at this moment time that their life changed forever. The twins' dad discovered that Christopher wasn't breathing. Chaos ensued and Christopher was rushed to the hospital, where he was pronounced dead.

A Map of Hope for the Lost

The Johnson family, Orlando, FL (2015)

The world swirled around Chelsea and her husband, Kwesi. The noise, the craziness...all seemed to sit on top of them. The world looked different and could never be the same.

Around that time, the dad, Kwesi, lost his job and the family was struggling. They needed help and needed others to step up to support them financially, emotionally, physically and spiritually. Their world was rocked. You will see in the following pages how the Johnson's were helped.

A Mother Knows She is in Need, But Can't Say What Would Help

Like the Johnson Family, I could not find any support or anyone to guide me through all the things I had to go through when Finley died. I didn't know what I needed, but I knew I needed help. I needed someone to walk me through all the things I had to navigate through after her death.

However, there was almost no help to be found at that time. Because there has been so little comprehensive support for families after loss, Jillian, whom I referenced before, is very passionate about guiding families into help and creating spaces for families to communicate/share.

Jillian has helped facilitate support groups for mothers after loss for many years. As an educator and a mom who experienced loss herself, Jillian offers a unique perspective to both the support group attendees in her area as well as for her social services students. She is able to paint the picture as to why support is so valuable and needed after loss:

"Bereaved parents need family, friends, colleagues, and community members to provide assistance with meals, laundry, house cleaning, and grocery shopping, just to name a few. They also need a comforting space for others to listen and sit in silence if needed. Many bereaved parents want others to say their baby's name and acknowledge that their baby mattered to others. After a few days, maybe weeks, almost everyone goes back to their 'normal' lives, but bereaved parents are left feeling hopeless, isolated, and caught between having to deal with difficult emotions and juggle day-to-day tasks like working, caregiving, housekeeping, etc. It is very challenging, as a bereaved parent, to watch the world continue to move forward, when they are stuck in the deepest suffering. Bereaved parents need their friends, family, and community support so that they can move through the acute grief with connection, love, and acknowledgement. They need to feel understood and validated so that their grief is witnessed."

Heart, Mind. and Body Wounds

From what I've learned in medical journals as well as from my own experience, grief affects not only the emotional parts of a person, but the physical as well. Mothers' bodies are physically affected with a healthy delivery, but the same applies to a delivery where the child has passed away. From painful C-section surgeries, the natural deliveries, back pain, weight gain, etc, grieving mothers experience it all.

A mother's milk also comes in and makes the process physically and emotionally painful for the hurting mother. The food, sustenance that should have provided for her beautiful baby, now serves as a reminder of all that she lost. "There are ways grief negatively affects a mother that many don't realize. The mood irregularities that occur after a healthy delivery also affect a mother who loses a child. Post-Partum Mood Disorder affects both mothers whose babies comes out alive, along with mothers who babies are not living," said Jillian.

When a child dies, the confusion and fogginess make functioning almost impossible. To research, then pick up a phone to try and get help is extremely taxing and overwhelming. I went through this and didn't want any other mother or family to not have help thinking when they are unable to think.

What Hurts, What Helps

Both counseling and my Griefshare groups were incredibly helpful. In my support group, I started talking through all that I was going through. I heard other people's stories and felt less alone and overwhelmed. I needed to know I could make it.

I realized that when people are going through early trauma and pain, they need to hear that it isn't always so hard or always so bad. Death (and certainly the loss of a child) is unlike any other traumatic event. The death of a child is something that one can never truly "get over" or "make better." It is a forever thing, so for someone going through the death of a child, for years, they may need to hear things that validate what they are feeling and sometimes saying out loud. No matter how much time has passed, they are completely right to say "it's awful' or "it doesn't make sense" or "it's the worst feeling in the world." Empathy with infant loss is key to helping.

Here is something that you may assume would be helpful to a grieving mom, but I don't think so: talking about "the reason" it happened. You have one or more theories and whether right or wrong, don't try and talk about it with the mom. Just listen if she wants to talk about her own theory. Just listen if she says something, whether you agree or disagree. Don't point out her flawed logic. Don't tell her not to blame herself or anyone. Just listen, because it's a natural part of her process, trying desperately to make sense out of something that makes no sense. Don't try to help by steering her thoughts or offering your own explanation… because you really don't know. A few things you could say *instead* of offering theories:

"It's awful."

"It doesn't make any sense".

"It sucks".

"I don't get it".

"I'm sorry".

Emily Graham, a bereaved parent and grief writer, shares: "When my son died, I received a lot of advice. I found people do not know what to say. They default to the things they have been conditioned to say during these times. It came from many different sources, most of which had never lost a child. The advice came from good intentions, but it was hollow. Not at all what I needed in that moment." She also shared what things said to her made her pain twist into anger. "Trust that this is God's Plan." and "Give it time…time heals all wounds." Graham said that much of the input she received felt like pressure towards a direction someone else thought was best for her…"from someone that had never stood where I was standing."

Graham also has this advice:

4 Sympathy Messages to Avoid:

1. *I know how you feel.* Everyone experiences grief differently. It is best in this situation to just avoid this statement.

2. *This happened for a reason.* Even said in good intentions, anything like this should be avoided.

3. *It will be OK.* This can sound like you are making light of their grief. It will never be OK for them that their loved one is gone.

4. *Religious statements.* Unless you know the person shares your exact beliefs, it is best to avoid religion. After a great loss, many people question their faith. While that may seem like the perfect time to encourage them, it can cause anger or guilt. What may make you feel comforted, may not have the same effect on someone else.

Expectations: Don't Have Any

While not having unrealistic expectations is always a good practice in any relationship or situation, it is crucial when you want to be supportive to a mother who has lost a child. Some common expectations that well-meaning people have: assuming that the mother wants to be distracted from her pain by visiting or going out to a movie or dinner; thinking that the mom will respond to kind gestures with the usual signs of appreciation; expecting that the grieving mom will feel better after a few weeks.

By noticing and curtailing your expectations (even little ones), you can avoid feeling disappointed, confused, or unappreciated. When you have those feelings, they leak out and cause the helpless mom to feel guilty, disappointed in herself, resentful, or just overwhelmed. Certainly not what you intended!

Expectations can develop easily, so you have to be extra aware. They are pictures in your mind about how things should or will go or used to be. Some of them stem from thinking that you know what the mother needs. No, you don't…not like I do, after going through the grief myself as well as talking with hundreds of other moms as my team and I helped them during grieving.

When you're not busy with the expectation pictures in your mind, you can be present. This means that you are more able to just be there for your friend or family member. But, the most important expectation to NOT have is to think that she can tell you what she needs, how you and others can support her, what would be most helpful. No, don't expect that from her. She can't think, she can't imagine *anything* working to relieve the pain she feels, and she can't articulate a clear request of you or anyone.

Thank goodness she has you to think for her. Fortunately, my work with hundreds of bereaved mothers through The Finley Project has led me and my team of experts to develop what CAN help. These steps and tools are especially for you. In the next chapter, you'll see the proven and practical things you can use to be of immense support to any grieving mom, starting today.

More Than "I'm Sorry"

CHAPTER 8

My Daughter's Forever Legacy: The Finley Project®

I choose to believe that Finley's death is minor compared to the legacy of her life. It has great meaning because I allowed it to inspire me to help mothers heal after loss and also equip others with how to help. I'm also working on how to help ensure that mothers have better hospital care, care that could prevent the loss of their child.

The Finley Project is a tribute to the little life of my daughter Finley. I am honored to share in more detail my journey with the Project and also my commitment to advocating for hospital staffing changes.

Starting The Finley Project was one of the hardest, yet most rewarding things I have ever done in my entire life. I was determined to do whatever possible so that no other woman would have to go through what I went through.

One of my favorite quotes by Ayn Rand is, "The question isn't who is going to let me; it's who is going to stop me?"

During the first six months after the loss of my daughter, I was grateful for the handful of people who stepped up to support me. Each was generous with their compassion and caring, but it was clear that I also needed professional help. My friends cared enough to direct me to the right counselor and support groups. Initially, I needed others to think for me, since I couldn't think for myself.

When I began channeling my devastation and frustration into a force for good (helping other moms), I started an extensive search, looking to see where and how others get help. When my results were so nominal, I did more research, talked with medical professionals, and called community groups including churches. I couldn't believe the absence of resources and lack of support in our area as well as around the country.

I can only imagine that this is because a grieving mother's pain is hard to understand and see, since a broken heart is hidden inside her traumatized body and spirit. It's imperative that families, friends, and the community step up to help, because the lack of direction on top of heavy grief is debilitating. Those who sense that the mother needs support and are ready and willing to help don't really know what to do, what kind of support is needed, and what could have the unintended result of not being helpful at all. Families and friends need someone to guide them. I learned the hard way that sufficient support was sorely missing.

Once I could summon the strength to try and be helpful to others, my heart broke for the mothers coming out of our local area hospitals who did not have anyone helping them or guiding them where to go or what to do. A majority of the time, hospital staff tries to prepare a family for the mother being discharged, but a family is never really ready or equipped. In my personal experience along with professional experience, I've seen that even if the hospital provides supportive suggestions or resources, the family doesn't hear it or forgets it before they get home. I've also seen cases where a family did not receive any direction or support as to what to do when discharged.

In the study "Pregnancy and Infant Loss: A Survey of Families' Experiences," when participants were asked about being given discharge or follow-up instructions from healthcare providers, "23% indicated they were given no instruction, while 8% indicated they did not remember if they were or not. When people received discharge or follow-up instructions, verbal (55%) and written instructions (29%) were most common." (Watson *et al. BMC Pregnancy and Childbirth*, 2019)

Education = Saving Lives

In addition to helping hundreds of grieving mothers, I have spent years continually educating hospital staff—NICU nurses, Social Workers, Neonatologists, Palliative care departments—on the importance of connecting a family right away to support so they can have the tools to lean on initially and as the "fog starts to lift."

It is imperative for a family to have a smooth handoff from the hospital to the home for a variety of reasons. This includes medical follow-up appointments, support group information, and organizations that specialize in grief support. The handoff and personal connection is important for the hospital staff to make to help eliminate confusion and additional disorientation for the mother and father.

In the *American Journal of Hospice and Palliative Medicine* (Brooten, 2012), "Parent's Perceptions of Health Care Providers Actions Around Child ICU Death: What Helped, What Did Not," the study shows that "after the death, parents often feel lost and abandoned by health care providers and want to continue the relationship with hospital staff." In an already traumatic and bewildering, life-altering event, families want to and hope that their medical team will not only connect them directly to both clinical care and mental health support, but also to have some follow up from the hospital team. Mothers and father want to know that they are not also abandoned by the staff and hospital system as a whole.

Unfortunately, a smooth handoff and follow-up care by hospitals does not always happen for a variety of reasons, some of which include: a lack of education, physician/medical burnout, lack of manpower, frequent staff changes, lack of dedicated staff, and so forth. Due to this gap in care, the need for family and friends to step up and guide a mother and fathers after loss is incredibly important.

My Commitment Pulled Me Out of My Comfort Zone

I had never felt so sure about anything in my life: I was out to make a difference. I was going to develop and put in place a reliable system to help grieving mothers by providing practical, meaningful support. I realized that in order to really help in a big way, I would need to establish a nonprofit organization.

Starting The Finley Project was hard and took time. I waited a year after Finley died to officially launch the organization. Even during that year, I was regularly attending counseling sessions and Griefshare support groups. I had to maintain my own healing journey while figuring out how to help others.

I knew I needed to learn a lot about the nonprofit sector including how to set one up, how to raise support, how to create a budget, a website, and a multitude of infrastructure details that were outside of my past experience. I ended up enrolling into a Nonprofit Certification Program, receiving a "Certification in Nonprofit Management" and later, an additional "Certification in Leadership Development."

I started to meet with others in the nonprofit sector and people that were serving the under-served, as well. I found it difficult to relate to many leaders in the nonprofit sector since most were not original founders, encountering everything for the first time and developing everything from the ground up, but there were many nuggets of helpful tools and tips that helped.

I scoured the internet for organizations serving grieving families across the country. I talked to support group leaders, children's grief organizations, NICU palliative care doctors and other medical professionals. I wanted to determine if what I saw in my community was true for the rest of the country—a lack of a formal program to help step-by-step. Sadly, I found almost nothing was organized for this purpose. Many communities did not have a comprehensive program by any means, nor a monthly support group.

After this conclusion, I settled on the concept of helping mothers from the time a loss happens all the way through five years after. I wanted to help a mom with the practical, the emotional, and the mental/spiritual aspects of her grief journey. My intention was to find a way to help any mom in any and all communities. I knew this had to be designed to care for the whole person, also known as a "Holistic Approach." This meant that we would need to be hand-in-hand with the mom, leading and guiding her through her journey of grieving and healing after losing a child.

The Finley Project Model was designed to "think" for the grieving mother when she can't think for herself. The organization was officially launched on Finley's "1st birthday" at a Celebration of Life event in July 2014. This was the funeral that Finley never had, since I couldn't seem to handle all the things I had to when she died (especially with her father absent.) It seemed to satisfy myself and others at the time to simply commit to having a ceremony later, on her first birthday. This eventually became a big Celebration of Life event and the official launch date of the nonprofit organization that honors her life.

My Daughter's Forever Legacy: The Finley Project®

Finley's Celebration of Life, Winter Park, FL (2014)

From that point forward, the Celebration of Life event continued each year and now serves as a day of remembering and raising support for The Finley Project program.

Developing an Excellent Model

Understanding a mother's needs was a learned process and designing The Finley Project was quite challenging. There were many, many tears along the way, but after some time, the pros certainly outweighed the cons.

I developed the program aligned with "Maslow Theory" in the "Maslow's Hierarchy of Needs." The Hierarchy takes the form of a triangle or pyramid shape, representing what humans need in order to be able to move towards self-actualization. The theory shows that the needs of people had to be met from the bottom upwards, and that the lower four layers were all *deficiency* or *lower-order* needs – so that, for example, a person who doesn't have enough food would not be focused on needs relating to the *higher level* such as self-realizations/self-work (https://counsellingtutor.com/counselling-approaches/person-centred-approach-to-counselling/maslow-hierarchy-of-needs/).

Maslow's Hierarchy of Needs

The Finley Project was developed to not only provide the basic "survival" needs for families such as food and meals, but to truly earn a families' trust, leading to connecting them with the resources and support they most need.

Moving someone into a counseling environment when they are apprehensive about it in the first place is difficult, but if trust is earned through providing basic things, a person is more likely to eventually focus on self-care such as counseling if suggested by the trusted entity.

The main purpose of this book is to share with every family or anyone who cares about a grieving mother, anywhere in the world, The Finley Project 7-Part Holistic Program. This is how to help a mother and father after loss. In fact, it is the best, most comprehensive and proven program of its kind anywhere in the country, and probably the world. Following is your step-by-step guide which I am encouraging you to use to make a difference. It will. You can.

CHAPTER 9

The Finley Project
7-Part Holistic Model and Program

It may have happened suddenly, without any warning. Or you may have watched in agony as your sister, friend, neighbor, co-worker or other family member walked through the tearful journey of their child's illness. Each situation is different, but when someone you care about is hurting, you hurt, too.

Losing a child is nothing short of traumatic. It's nothing one can prepare for. Your heart aches for the grieving mom and you are desperate to help, but how? You and your friends, family, co-workers are feeling helpless, even useless, maybe even afraid to do the wrong thing, say the wrong thing. You want to offer something, more than words, more than "I'm Sorry." By using the following action-step tool, The Finley Project Model®, you can make a difference that will be constructive immediately and also long-term.

Who is this tool for?

- You want to help a woman and her family get through the nightmare that no one should have to go through alone.

- You don't want to waste your own efforts and energy doing things that won't help much, if at all.

- You understand that the grieving mother does not know and cannot communicate what she needs.

- You want to know what having all the bases covered means and you are willing to ask others to cover them.

- You are eager to help others see exactly how they can best help, since many people are at a loss or afraid to do something that could make matters worse.

- You want to be educated and well-equipped now, even if the need is not imminent, so if something happens down the road you will be empowered to be a competent helper.

- You are a leader who comes in contact with grieving families and wants a proven, life-changing tool to utilize in your role as a counselor, church or civic group leader, hospital administrator or chaplain, or grief support group leader.

- You commit to being the go-person, the central volunteer who will communicate to others what is needed, by when, and how to accomplish it (which is ALL right here in this book for you!).

The following pages are to teach and guide you through actionable steps you can take, knowing that our organization's approach and Model has helped many, many grieving mothers in meaningful ways.

Proven Steps: Actions to Take—Mistakes to Avoid

The Finley Project Model® will be your powerful, effective, and highly-specialized tool. It's a great idea to invite others to partner with you to utilize these strategies. In fact, it's imperative. This multi-faceted approach needs a community, a team, given the nature of help needed.

Most everyone is unaware of how to best help and would appreciate actionable steps and ideas. You can help them support the grieving mother whom they care about. You can gather together, pool resources, and follow the process. So, please follow along to learn more how your family, friend group, civic group, coworkers, church congregation, synagogue, or neighborhood group can make a difference in helping someone who is in the throes of loss.

It's important to remember, "it's a marathon, not a sprint," when it comes to helping a person navigate through a painful loss. There is no one experience that defines "grief." Everyone goes through it differently, depending on their own belief system, their relationship with their deceased loved one, the strength of their personal resilience, and especially the support they have around them.

The Finley Project 7-Part Holistic Model and Program

I will show you here why this unique, real-world Model which I developed matters, how much it costs to support a hurting person, and how to help, step-by-step.

The Finley Project Model®

How Others Can Help Others

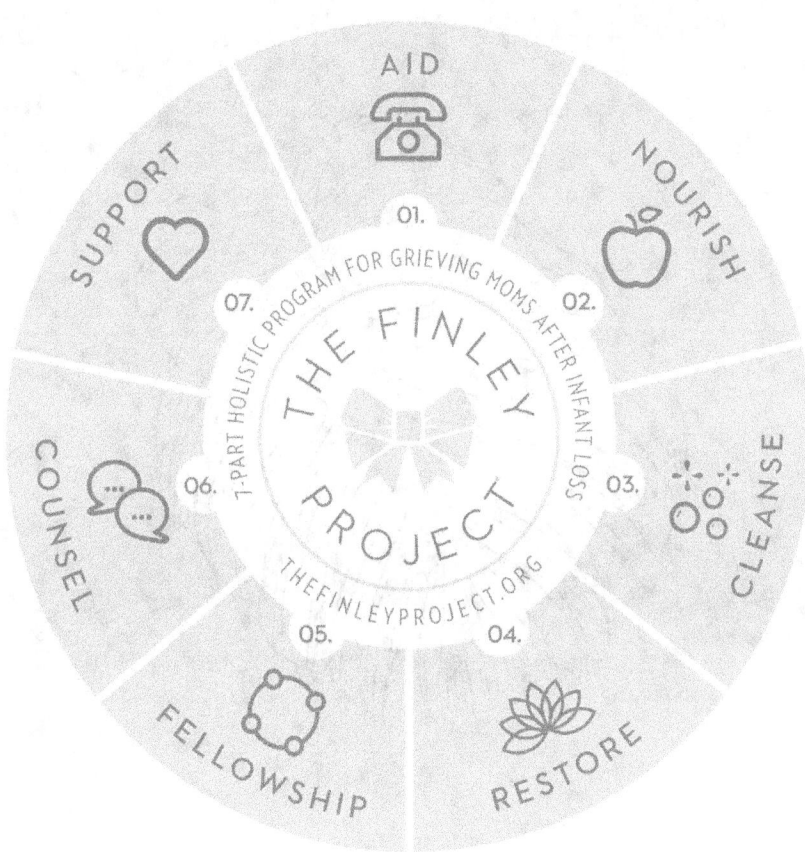

Chart 1.1

More Than "I'm Sorry"

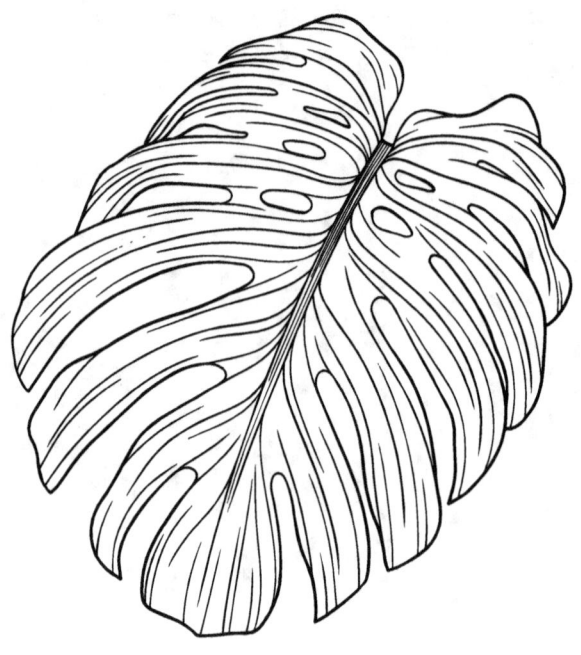

The Finley Project Model®

The Finley Project Model® has been utilized through The Finley Project Program since 2013. It was developed to help mothers who lost an infant at any time between 22 weeks' gestation and two years of age. The Model has helped women who lost an infant due to various genetic issues, accidents, medical malpractice incidents, and other causes. (Sample: [Chart 1.2])

No	Date Enrolled	State	Condition/Reason
1	11/14/14	FL	Stillbirth
2	8/11/14	FL	Malpractice
3	1/7/15	NC	Hole in Heart
4	11/27/14	NC	Stillbirth
5	11/1/14	FL	Trisomy 18
6	9/23/14	FL	Stillbirth
7	4/27/15	FL	SIDS
8	5/14/15	FL	Stillbirth
9	4/24/15	FL	SIDS
10	8/7/15	FL	Cancer
11	9/28/15	FL	Stillbirth
12	10/26/15	NC	Cord Accident
13	10/18/15	FL	Encephala
14	3/6/15	CO	Premature
15	8/20/15	TX	Premature
16	1/4/16	FL	Premature
17	10/18/15	FL	Malpractice

No	Date Enrolled	State	Condition/Reason
18	6/30/15	NC	Campomelic Dysplasia
19	11/9//15	FL	Trisomy 18
20	1/29/16	FL	Stillbirth
21	11/16/15	FL	Stillbirth
22	2/16/16	FL	Premature
23	2/18/16	NC	Trisomy 18
24	2/15/16	LA	Congenial Heart Defect
25	4/16/16	MI	Stillbirth
26	4/13/16	PA	Krabbe Disease
27	4/26/16	NC	Stillbirth
28	4/27/16	NC	Premature
29	4/27/16	FL	Premature
30	5/10/16	WV	Trisomy 18

Chart 1.2

The Finley Project Model was designed to "think" for the grieving mother when they couldn't think for themselves immediately after or shortly after the loss of a child. The Model also addresses the "whole" person—therefore, it is considered to be the nation's only Holistic Program for Mothers After Infant Loss. What makes The Finley Project Model stand out among other Models is that it is all encompassing, where a person is assisted early with practical/physical needs and then the emotional/spiritual needs are supported long-term.

When a death occurs, grief naturally takes over, but unfortunately the "to-do" list has just begun. The way The Finley Project Model* begins is by offering someone practical/physical support with a funeral, meal gift cards, and even house cleaning services. These initial things are very important for many reasons. By handling the practical needs, you are helping to ease physical, mental and emotional burdens in the early days after loss.

The best "more than I'm sorry" support to provide is taking care of pressing tasks which are just too big a burden for a grieving mom or family. No one is prepared for this kind of loss. No "pre-planned funeral arrangements" have been set up, for example. The funeral planning support is something that most families can't even fathom having to deal with. By stepping in to handle logistics and helping to create honoring elements, stress is eased on the family.

Funeral Planning Support along with Meal Gift Cards, House Cleaning and Massage Therapy—allow those helping the grieving person the opportunity to gain or continue to build trust with the person they are supporting. These are things that show one cares without requiring too much from the hurting person. This is love in action.

The long-term goal is to provide spiritual/emotional support through counseling and support group placement as well as connecting them to someone that has walked a similar journey. The initial practical/physical components help earn their trust and build loyalty while the spiritual/emotional components help provide tools and support for long-term healing.

The Finley Project Model is Comprised of Seven Parts

1. AID: Planning the Funeral/Celebration of Life
2. NOURISH: Meal or Grocery Gift Cards
3. CLEANSE: House Cleaning
4. RESTORE: Massage Therapy

} Physical/Practical

5. COUNSEL: Licensed Mental Health Counseling
6. FELLOWSHIP: Support Group Placement
7. SUPPORT: Support from Volunteers

} Spiritual/Emotional

The Finley Project Model® Cost Breakdown

Depending on the state, city, and other factors, the expenses herein are approximates based on our experience, but will undoubtedly rise with time. The costs, without funeral expenses, are approximately $1500. As seen through The Finley Project Model, the cost breakdown is as such:

The Finley Project: Cost per Mom w/Full Program Involvement			
Type of Support	Cost per day	Total days	Total costs
Professional Cleaning	$100	3	$300
Meal & Grocery Gift Cards	$25	7	$175
Licensed Mental Health Counseling	$70	12	$840
Massage Therapy	$60	3	$180
Total			$1,495
Cost to sponsor a mom			$1,495

The Overview of Cost should give those wanting to help an idea of what needs to be raised and collected in order to meet these critical needs. The costs vary based on locale and providers used, but these variances and alternatives will be discussed throughout each Step.

There are many ways to raise and gather support. Be creative and don't be afraid to ask! Be sure to highlight what the money raised is going to SPECIFICALLY. Some support raising suggestions:

- Gofundme or other internet-based fundraising platforms
- Car Wash
- Small event – Bingo Night, Cornhole Tournament, Poker Tournament
- Garage Sale
- Bake Sale
- Pancake Breakfast
- Virtual silent auction (one resource is https://www.32auctions.com

As You Use This Model…

Each Step notes the actions which our Model has proven to be the most practical and helpful ways to support a grieving mom. Are there other things that can be done? YES! If one of the actions doesn't seem to fit your situation, look for alternatives to accomplish something that helps in that Step. Also, I developed a Care Guide for you if you would like more in-depth guidance for every Step, checklists, and info pages you can fill in to help you stay organized and on track with each Step.

The companion book, *More than "I'm Sorry" CARE GUIDE*, is available on Amazon.com, Barnes & Noble, and all major online booksellers.

More Than "I'm Sorry"

(1)
AID

When you think of "AID," think "Assistance In Dealing." Helping someone after loss is why you are here and one of the first ways that assistance is needed is with Funeral Planning. Just when a grieving mother feels like sleeping her day away or whatever gets her through each hour, she is going to be asked to make certain decisions. This is an area where you can step in and walk through the details with her, assisting her through the Funeral Planning process.

> "An ask or pressure for any decision can feel extremely overwhelming. A mom doesn't know which way is up and needs AID in planning the hardest funeral she will ever attend."
>
> Noelle Moore, a mom who's been there

Example of How to Help Aid:

Funeral Planning

Why is support through Funeral Planning important?

The truth is that no one has a funeral plan already set up for a little child. Cute nursery at home, yes—funeral arrangements, no. Making the call to a funeral home feels impossible to a family. But it must be done. Understandably, the parents are not in any condition to deal with this, yet their input and wishes need to be heard and honored.

You can suggest that a *Celebration of Life* be held at a later time, even a year or two down the road, or on the child's birthday, but that is just an option in contrast or in conjunction with a funeral shortly thereafter. Some of the most beneficial words I have ever shared with a grieving family are, "Don't feel like you have to do everything and anything during their funeral. You can have a special *Celebration of Life* in a year or two so you have time to plan it out and have it fully express everything you want. It's okay to wait to do something down the road."

You want to remove the pressure of trying to honor the deceased infant in every way which is overwhelming. This is not the end of this person's memory or honoring them.

A helper can talk to a funeral home, relay the parents' wishes, set up the logistics. What specifically can you do?

For a more traditional Funeral Ceremony:

- Offer to help go through her wishes and create an agenda of what to include for the day—people to ask to speak; songs, poems or scripture, and other meaningful things.

- Offer to have a beautiful program created such as Cherished Prints–www.cherished-prints.com/shop/. These are customized programs that are beautifully put together.

- Offer to help plan the meal after the ceremony.

- Offer to help set up/plan an honor space/table.

For a Celebration of Life:

- Offer to plan the event – i.e., BBQ, nice dinner, get-together.

- Set up the food – catering, potluck, cooking on site, etc.

- Offer to help go through her wishes and create an agenda of what to include for the day—people to ask to speak; music, poems or scripture, and other meaningful things.

- Offer to have a beautiful program created such as Cherish Prints–www.cherished-prints.com/shop/. These are customized programs that are beautifully put together.

- Offer to purchase butterflies for a release, or lanterns.

- Offer an Honor Space/table. This space can include pictures, favorite items, memories.

- One idea that's special is to have rocks laid out and guests sign the rocks. The rocks can then be placed in a container and later placed in a garden.

More Than "I'm Sorry"

(2) NOURISH

Like an extremely wilted plant, a grieving mom is in dire need of nourishment. At first, we can't worry about her blossoming—that comes much later. For now, we just need to support her with an infusion of nourishment. It's not that hard to provide, but don't expect her to recognize how much she needs it. A grieving mother is not typically worried about food and eating and helping her stay nourished is a great gift.

Example of How to Help Nourish:

Meal Delivery & Grocery Gift Cards

Why are Meal & Grocery Gift Cards important? When I first started The Finley Project, I remember being eager to offer counseling to families. However, after my daughter Finley's death, the first family I knew to lose an infant was not open to counseling right away. The mother said, "I appreciate your willingness to help me and get me into counseling, but I can't even think about that right now. I had to stay in a Ronald McDonald house while my child was in the NICU for three months. Now I'm home and I have to manage my household pretty much by myself. I can barely get food on the table or have the money to buy groceries. I just need some basic help first."

A light went off for me then. I realized that people need to feel safe, secure, and cared for within their home first before they can engage in counseling. It became clear that The Finley Project needed to help the family first with the basics, including food.

A mother in The Finley Project program shared, "I received the gift cards. This was so appreciated by our family since dinner time is not the best time anymore. I've lost a lot of my interest in cooking since my daughter died…You are an amazing group of people. I hope to one day help a woman in this situation like you do. Thank you for your generosity and support!"

A lot of people decide to bring food to a grieving family which is a wonderful gesture. This can be done utilizing a scheduling platform such Meatltrain.com. This platform allows others to sign up for various meals and days. When doing this, please let the grieving family know this is being done and also that you will ask those doing the meals to leave the food in a place by the front door or on the porch (like in a large cooler).

Most grieving people do not want to have to socialize or "welcome" people into their home right after loss. It's important to let those know who are delivering food that their generous and caring hearts are appreciated, but the family is not yet ready for visitors. People may actually feel relieved that all they need to do is drop off the food, that more is not expected.

Another option, if meals are not something that can be done, is to purchase grocery Gift Cards. The Finley Project found that Target or Walmart Gift Cards were most helpful as it allowed families to purchase food, toiletries or other items. Other options for Gift Cards include – pizza delivery, fast food or local restaurants that deliver. Often families do not feel like getting out but are happy to have a meal delivered. Gift Cards are a wonderful option even if there is a Mealtrain set up as it allows families to use them to go where they want to go or have what they want to have delivered on their own time. A mother in The Finley Project program shared:

> "I received the gift cards. This was so appreciated by our family since dinner time is not the best time anymore. I've lost a lot of my interest in cooking since my daughter died and now losing another child, it is very rare when I cook dinner anymore. You guys are an amazing group of people. I hope to one day help a woman in this situation…"
>
>  A mom who received our "Nourishment"

Restaurant and Grocery Gift Cards ensure that every mother and her family have hot meals and a stocked refrigerator.

Alternative:

Plan a less formal schedule for the long haul by assigning a few friends, over three months to bring a large meal, one time a week to remind the family they are cared for and loved. Providing a meal once a week allows a family to have leftovers and enjoy the meal two or more days. This longer-term approach helps with food after others may have stopped providing meals.

More Than "I'm Sorry"

(3) CLEANSE

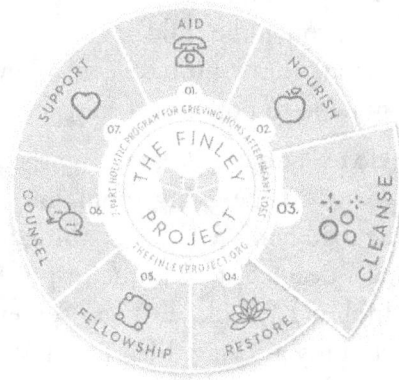

>  "A clean and ordered environment helps a grieving mom begin to order her own internal space."
>
> Noelle Moore, a mom who's been there

Example of How to Help Cleanse:

House Cleaning

Why is House Cleaning important? As a mother grieves, simple daily tasks like cooking and cleaning are overwhelming. Housekeeping services provide a clean and healthy environment, but also relieve a burden or guilt/pressure to do what she used to keep up with easily.

A family member or close friend can help just by getting all the piled-up dishes and kitchen cleaned, or fold all the laundry, or make the mother's bathroom sparkle. Anything helps.

Sometimes a mom prefers a stranger to do the cleaning—she doesn't want to feel embarrassed or uncomfortable. Ask if she's ever used a maid or cleaning service she liked. Pay for them to come. Or, hire a service you are familiar with and trust. You want to be certain this is stress-free for the mom. Take her to lunch or to a quiet lake/park while her house is getting cleaned if you like.

VERY IMPORTANT NOTE: Do not take it upon yourself or let anyone touch the child's belongings or remove any "sad memories." The grieving mom must have control over this process. It can do more harm than good to not respect this.

Taylor Gaythe, a Program mother, shared, "We had all of Benjamin's toys out in the living room since that's where we spent most of our time together. We left everything untouched for probably a month and then I decided it was time to put things away. We had people offer to help, but I felt like this was something I needed to do on my own as part of my grieving. I felt like if we allowed someone else to do that, we wouldn't process that part of him being gone."

Taylor Gaythe, Orlando, FL (2022)

Another Program mother, Joanna Lynch, shared, "While I was at the hospital, I had a friend go stay with my pets. I asked her to box everything up and put it away before I got home. I thought it would be too hard to see it. This was a huge mistake. A few others came over and cleared my son's room out completely and ended up putting his stuff in the attic. Coming home to an empty room and knowing his stuff was up there killed me. I made my husband go up and take it all back down. It's still in boxes in his closet and I still like to go in there and sit in the recliner and hold some of his things. I don't really plan on ever getting rid of it. I hope one day I can share it with a sibling of his and use it to remember him by."

Erica Dameron received the terrible news that her child would not be born alive, yet she had to go through the birthing process. Months later, she said, "While I was at the hospital waiting to give birth to my daughter, Peyton, I had some friends offer to go to my house and pack up her room. This infuriated me. I hadn't even given birth to her yet and people were wanting to erase her from my house. I know they were just trying to be helpful, but it was extremely hurtful. Once I got home, I didn't really touch her things for a few months."

Another Program mom, Elizabeth Romero, told us, "I keep some of her items in my closet, right next to my stuff. It's a daily reminder of her and brings me comfort to see her little shoes and onesie next to my clothes. Her stuff reminds me she existed and is my child, even if she never got to wear them."

If you are rather surprised to know how some mothers feel about their child's belongings, you are not alone. How could you guess this? Many moms say that people incorrectly assume that the things which trigger memories of the child should be out of sight. As one mom put it, "Why? Do they think I would completely forget this ever happened? As if hiding a car seat or little blanket would allow me to forget?"

> "It is proven that an important part of a grieving person's healing process is going through the deceased loved one's belongings when they are ready."
>
> Noelle Moore, a mom who's been there

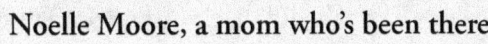

This process can sometimes take months if not years to walk through.

The Cleanse Step is therefore *not the task of cleaning out a deceased child's things*; it is for handling any typical cleaning and organizing that the mother would normally be able to do. This Step helps the mom in many ways—it can give her a sense that there's order.

To offer cleaning, all logistics will need to be handled. Assuming she does not already use or know of a particular cleaning company she wants, you will need to find one.

Here are some suggestions when starting the process of figuring out cleaning for the grieving person:

Is there a national chain in their area? Why a national chain?

- They are licensed/insured and make a person feel more comfortable than a local company.
- They often work with organizations that handle complex medical issues and can be more sensitive to what you are trying to do.
- Note that they often don't work on the weekends or at night.
- Don't be afraid to tell them that the cleaning is for someone that lost a child or loved one. Feel free to let them know the person may be very sensitive to items in the home that they would not like touched.

  For example, we once had a mother whose 2-year-old daughter, on her last day alive, had placed her sticky little hands on the sliding glass doors. This mother requested that the glass not be cleaned.

  Another example: A mother had been breastfeeding her premature baby while in the NICU, but once he died, the mother left all the bottles, bottle brush, and breast pump in a certain place on the counter. She asked that the cleaning company not move or touch these items. She was not yet ready to change a moment in time that had been before her baby son died.

- Never schedule a cleaning company to show up as a surprise to the mom. Get her input, ask what day of the week she prefers, and assure her that any special instructions such as what not to touch will be clarified.
- Tell the company you want three 1-hour cleanings over the course of three months.
- Ask if the mother or grieving person can call and ask questions about what can and can't be cleaned.
- The company will need a credit card on file.
- Make sure the day before they are scheduled for the cleaning that you confirm the appointment and that they have your payment info on file. This is important!

(3) CLEANSE

Some of the mothers felt a sense of great relief when the Cleanse Step was taken care of. Ashley Schimmer shared that after her son Lincoln died: "The cleaning ladies just did an amazing, fantastic job as always! Thank you so very much. Having a clean home is so I nice. It is hard finding motivation to go dust, mop, etc., the whole house, but specifically.... in the nursery. One of the cleaning ladies, who has been cleaning since the first visit, offered to mop and dust in my baby Lincoln's room today. ☺ It made my heart so happy! I got to show off his room and pictures. It made me burst with pride getting to talk about our Lincoln. She really went above and beyond! Walking inside my house from getting my daughter, it smelled so nice and fresh! After dreading Mother's Day this last week leading up to it & the lack of motivation for anything, my house greatly suffered. Having one less thing to worry about is such a relief! Thank You. Thank you."

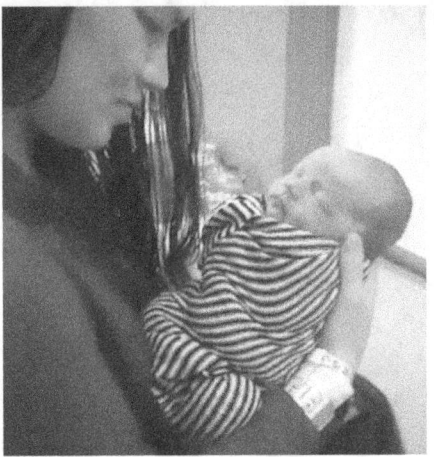

Ashley Schimmer & Lincoln, Orlando, FL (2016)

Alternative:

If a professional service is not available or cannot be afforded, an option is to gather a few friends together to clean the home for the person. This sometimes works as along as the person doesn't feel judged or uncomfortable. Sometimes a stranger (an outside cleaning company) is the best option as there is less room for shame/embarrassment. Other times, a group of friends helps to ease any uncomfortable feelings or uncertainty about a stranger in their home. Whoever is helping must be clear about the grieving mom's wishes such as whether something should be moved or touched at all.

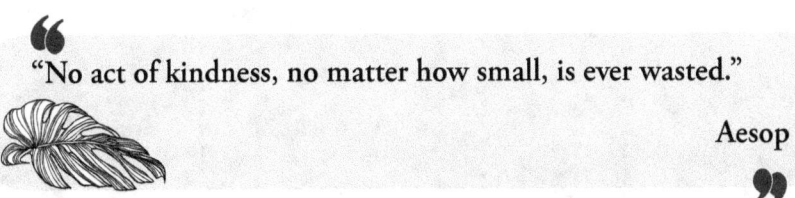

"No act of kindness, no matter how small, is ever wasted."

Aesop

More Than "I'm Sorry"

(4) RESTORE

>  "My heart felt broken and my body, too. I needed help being put back together...I needed to be restored. Massage therapy allowed me meaningful moments to feel like a whole person again. To feel worthy of time and touch made me feel more me again."
>
> Noelle Moore, a mom who's been there

Example of How to Help Restore:

Massage Therapy

Why is Massage Therapy important?

"The benefits of Massage are numerous especially when the recipient is in a state of grief. Grief is a prime contributor to stress and stress can have long-term effects on the body. Massage can assist with the physical and even emotional ramifications associated with grief."

—Erika and Michel Sasser, Owners, Massage Envy®

The first time I had a Massage after Finley died was the first time that an entire sixty minutes passed and I had not cried. Massage brought a sense of calm to my aching heart and an hour of rest that often wasn't possible during sorrow-filled nights.

Consider the five main health benefits of Massage Therapy according to the American Massage Therapy Association (AMTA). It is clear that each one of these are perfect ways to help a grieving mother.

1. Lowers stress—The effects of stress can take emotional and physical tolls. Massage Therapy can relieve stress and conditions associated with it, such as tension headaches.

2. Increase immune function—Massage Therapy can help boost immune system strength.

3. Boost mental health and wellness—Symptoms of stress, anxiety and depression (all associated with mental health) may be directly affected with Massage Therapy.

4. Manage pain—Pain can negatively affect a person's quality of life and impede recovery from illness or injury.

5. Improve physical fitness—Massage can reduce muscle tension, improve exercise performance and prevent injuries.

Remember, a grieving person is not capable of thinking, so your role is to think for them. You can ask the mom to choose three dates over the next one-to-three months that work for them. You or another helper can handle booking the appointments directly with the licensed massage provider. Be sure to pay in advance, including a gratuity, and remind the provider that all they need to say when their client checks out is, "It's all taken care of."

What's the action to take?

The Finley Project Model provides three Massage sessions that are given once a month for three months. The Finley Project Model used a national licensed Massage chain that is reputable and insured for comfortability.

When calling, you can let them know the following:

- You are calling on behalf of someone that has experienced a significant loss.

- You are looking to book three Massage appointments over three months for them.

(4) RESTORE

- You will be responsible for paying for the service AS well as gratuity. Please remind them that you do not want them asking for payment from the person at check-out.

- If the Massage provider does not ask you to complete a credit authorization form, you will be asked for payment over the phone. If you are comfortable do so, you can provide it at that time.

- You will need to provide the mother's phone number along with last name.

- Let the mom know they have appointments scheduled and the provider's location. Have her plug the info into her calendar or phone at that time, telling her to plan on arriving 15 minutes before the appointment to check in. Be sure they understand that they should not be asked to pay anything at the end of their session.

The average cost for Massage Therapy at a national chain is $50 for the first appointment for a new client, then a tip on top of the service of $12-$15 is recommended. After that, the second and third Massages often cost more, around $80-$90 a session, plus a $12-$15 tip. In total, the cost for the three Massages over a three months' time will cost your support team approximately $255-$275.

Alternative:

If a regular Licensed Massage Therapist is not an option due to cost, an alternative solution is a Massage Therapy School. The student therapists are well-trained and helpful, they just haven't gotten their credentials and license yet. They need a large number of hands-on hours and the fee is often drastically reduced.

Another option is to utilize the "Groupon" app, which may offer significantly discounted massage sessions with a licensed qualified therapist looking for new clients.

More Than "I'm Sorry"

(5) FELLOWSHIP

 "Many mothers feel alone and like they are the only ones feeling such deep pain and loss. Connecting a mother to a community of others going through similar losses can help greatly."

Noelle Moore, a mom who's been there

Example of Fellowship Support:

Support Group Placement

Why is a Support Group important? Feeling like she is not alone and is not the only one in the abyss of loss is critical for surviving, short-term and long-term.

Hope. The reason that being with others and hearing their stories, their ways of coping (or maybe not coping in some instances), is imperative is that this offers perspective and hope.

A Support Group is a good opportunity for a father or partner to join the mother to learn how to cope and support one another. Hearing from other couples and what they are facing can help both parent's process what they are going through.

Some mothers worry that hearing about others' grief would be overwhelming, or that talking about their story would be too triggering to their own pain. The fact is that once a mother shows up and give a support group a try, most of them come back. Support Groups are a safe space and create a sense of community. Mothers gather together with those rare people who have a real understanding of their particular kind of pain and grief. They find that in that group, they can share and be vulnerable. Support Groups reveal the unspoken things women and men are going through.

Some groups are virtual, others are in-person. Some are "drop-in" groups where a mother/father can attend at any time, while other groups are "closed" groups where one must register and attend for a set number of weeks. Then those group sessions are complete and usually a new group becomes open for both people who want to re-register as well as new participants.

A wonderful, weekly, in-person, closed group is GriefShare (https://www.griefshare.com), a Support Group program, that saved my life. The reason this group was so valuable was that it made me feel less alone and had a 13-week curriculum with action steps. In my particular group, the leaders were incredible as they greeted me with love and compassion. I can remember arriving to the church where the support group was located and could barely walk in. I was scared. However, instead of sitting back and waiting for the attendees to enter, the group leaders, Dale and Elaine Coulter, were waiting outside the room, welcoming me and directing me where to go. The comfort and peace these two life-saving leaders provided made me want to come back and participate.

Another group, **The Compassionate Friends,** provides hope and understanding to those who have lost a child at any age, due to any cause. https://www.compassionatefriends.org

Other Support Group options include virtual groups. Virtual groups have the benefit of convenience. Mothers usually don't feel up to driving themselves anywhere and there may not be easy transportation options for her. If you suggest a local group and she declines, ask her about a virtual one because that may be a good solution.

(5) FELLOWSHIP

Virtual Support Groups for Pregnancy and Infant Loss (Up To Age 1)

– **M.E.N.D. (Mommies Enduring Neonatal Death)** is a Christian, non-profit organization that reaches out to families who have suffered the loss of a baby through miscarriage, stillbirth, or early infant death. M.E.N.D. is a place for families to connect, share their unique story of loss, and learn to live life without your precious baby. https://www.mend.org

– **M.E.N.D. Nationwide Online Support Group** is a Christian, non-profit organization that reaches out to families who have suffered the loss of a baby through miscarriage, stillbirth, or early infant death. The group is on the third Thursday of each month at 8:00 p.m. Central. https://www.mend.org/nationwide-online-support-group

– **Share Pregnancy and Infant Loss Support** is a community for anyone in the family who has experienced the tragic loss of a baby. http://nationalshare.org/online-support

– **Star Legacy Foundation Online Support Group** provides live, online support groups for families who have experienced a perinatal loss. Groups are held via HIPAA-compliant videoconferencing and facilitated by trained health professionals. Registration is required only for the first time you attend. https://starlegacyfoundation.org/support-groups

– **TEARS Foundation** offers free support groups for bereaved families who have experienced the death of their baby. The groups are always open monthly to new members, and everyone is welcome to attend. Support for the deaf community and Spanish speaking community is also available. https://thetearsfoundation.org

Support Groups for Death of a Child at Any Age:

– **Bereaved Parents of the USA** provides a safe space where grieving parents and families can rebuild their lives after the death of a child. https://www.bereavedparentsusa.org

– **MISS Foundation** provides services to families who have experienced the death of a child at any age. https://missfoundation.org. They provide a free, 24/7, fully moderated online support group forums. Their moderators are fully trained and are also bereaved parents, grandparents, or siblings themselves. If you would like to join the forums, you'll need to apply for membership which will take 24 to 78 hours before it clears. If you'd like to apply to join the online support group: https://forums.missfoundation.org/login

Support Group for Sudden Infant Death Syndrome (SIDS) and Other Sleep-Related Infant Death:

– **First Candle** offers online support groups for those who have experienced loss by Sudden Infant Death Syndrome, stillbirth, and miscarriage.

Support Group for Sudden Unexplained Death in Childhood (SUDC), i.e., death in children between the ages of 1 and 18 years that remains unexplained after a thorough investigation, including an autopsy.

– **SUDC Foundation** offers resources and support for bereaved families who lost children due to sudden unexplained death.

For Children Who are Grieving:

Remember that older children of a mother who loses an infant are often suffering a traumatic loss of their "baby brother or sister" but their mom cannot be her usual comforting self.

– The National Alliance for Children's Grief (NACG) is a nonprofit organization that raises awareness about the needs of children and teens who are grieving a death and provides education and resources for anyone who supports them. Through the collective voice of our members and partners, we educate, advocate, and raise awareness about childhood bereavement. https://childrengrieve.org

Hospice Organizations – Hospice organizations have a variety of Support Groups for different types of losses.

Hospitals – Many hospitals have groups especially for those who have lost an infant or young child. Be sure to check ALL area hospitals, not just the one where the person was admitted, as groups are typically open to all people.

> "A support group saved my life."
>
>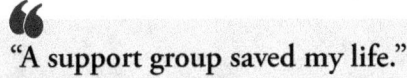
>
> Noelle Moore, a mom who's been there

If a Support Group is not available in the person's area, one of the best options is an online support group. Can't find one you think would be a good match? Organize one by using social media or connecting with hospice social workers, grief counselors, or church leaders.

More Than "I'm Sorry"

(6) COUNSEL

Example of Support through Counsel:

Licensed Mental Health Counseling

Why is Licensed Mental Health Counseling important? This service is probably the most important for a grieving mother, not only short-term, but for her long-term health. The counselor becomes a person's go-to support system for the months and years to come. Family and friends can only provide support as their own work, proximity, emotional health, and obligations allow. Counselors fill in the large gaps where others cannot and, most importantly, they are trained to address the intense psychological effects of having a child pass away.

Angela Sanders, a mother in The Finley Project Program, lost her son Milo to stillbirth. She shared how counseling helped her.

"The Finley Project helped me from the beginning. Noelle texted support the day of my son's funeral and it was so helpful to hear from someone who had survived. I desperately needed someone to tell me how to keep living and The Finley Project helped me kickstart a healthy direction. Counseling saved my life, my marriage, and made me feel less alone."

The Finley Project Counseling Philosophy: The Finley Project directs mothers to counseling providers immediately after a mother experiences the loss of an infant, up to 90 days after loss. The Finley Project program directs and pays for Counseling support that functions in the following ways:

- Counseling is provided as soon as possible to a mother, either through paying in full for sessions or paying for co-pays if the mother has an insurance benefit.

- Counseling is structured in such a way that it is intensive at first, 12 sessions weekly, then moves to a less frequent process after these initial 12 sessions. The initial 12 are paid for by The Finley Project. Next steps are to be determined by the counselor and mother after this period.

- Counseling services serve as a safeguard. Counselors provide the only clinical oversight for mothers in The Finley Project program. The Finley Project is the "concierge" in the process, coordinating the support and payment for the mothers for the counseling.

To help your grieving mother, this step is the one where you need to be persistent and persuasive. Yes, earlier steps must be addressed to help stabilize her home, but then she needs professional help. She may not agree. Here are some of the objections you may hear:

- "I don't need a counselor."
- "I've gone before, and it doesn't help."
- "I don't like my counselor."
- "I don't even know where to begin."
- "I can't afford it."

Help her find a counselor who has a lot of experience under his or her belt. Grief experience is a plus, such as if the counselor has lead grief support groups before, has counseled those going through grief, etc. There are some counselors that specialize in grief, but it's not a requirement. Tell the mom that all she must do is show up, she does not need to know how or what to talk about—the counselor will make her feel comfortable and lead the process.

Help her check with her insurance company to see what may be covered. Make a plan with the Support team to raise funds to cover what more is needed for at least three months. Also, check around in her community for free counseling offered through churches, colleges, and other organizations. Let's cover some of the most common questions my team and I hear.

Are there counselors that specialize in grief?

Yes, there are training and certifications that will give someone the title of a "Certified Grief Counselor." There are, however, even more important criteria when choosing a counselor. What you want to look for in a good grief counselor is a highly trained therapist who has the skills and tools to deal with the trauma of loss, which is complicated. You need a counselor that understands that the loss of a child is not only overwhelming in the present, but also devastates the vision of their family's future. Trying to find meaning in the chaos of losing a child can cause one or both parents to obsess over every past pregnancy decision and life choice.

Therapist Chris Kavenagh advises: "A good counselor will be able to hold and explore the past, present and future at the same time, while also instilling hope that the depth of what they feel today will not be what they feel forever. Grief is a very complicated journey and each mother needs to be treated as an individual and not a "process" that she has to get through. Having the skills to navigate, without fear, the convoluted, painful and sometimes chaotic state that is grief is what makes a good grief counselor." (Chris Kavenagh, LMHC, www.FiveStonesCounseling.com)

Should a mother's spouse or significant other go to counseling?

In 2014, I met a young woman from South Florida, who was hesitant about going to counseling and asked if her boyfriend could attend with her. I let her know that in our program, we want mothers to attend the first two to three sessions on their own, and then the spouse or significant other can join. This particular mother understood and went to the first counseling session. After that session, the mother disclosed that she was having major relational issues with her boyfriend and that she was thankful to have a safe place to talk over things with her counselor.

Although this is certainly not the case for everyone, it is often true that relationship tensions are high after any experience of significant loss. Whether verbalized or not, grieving people often feel that individual counseling offers a safe place to work through dealing with partners, family members, and others.

There are many instances on the flipside, where spouses and partners help each other immensely by going together. They have the chance to hear each other share and express things in a safe space to the counselor which they were hesitant to ask their partner about. If helpful, it is certainly okay for couples to go together to work through the loss, but at least one individual session for the mother initially is our recommendation.

She has insurance—can this be used for counseling?

Insurance coverage for counseling varies a lot, but there are ways you can help. First and foremost, have the mother call her insurance company and find out about her insurance benefits. Remember, she may be in a "brain fog" so much that she needs someone to be with her for that call (like beside her and the call is on "speaker"). That way, all the pertinent questions get asked on the call and all of the answers can be written down.

Some coverage includes only a few "free" sessions, while other plans cover an unlimited amount with a small copay. There is also coverage that provides sessions 100% at no charge. Another task to help her with is finding local providers who accept her insurance, which can be done over the phone or online on her insurance provider's website. From there, you could help by calling to see if they are taking new clients and if they have someone on staff that has worked with family's experiencing loss.

Where do we begin if our grieving mom has no insurance coverage for counseling?

Start by asking around, seeing what you can find out through word-of-mouth. You may learn that there are counselors that others have used that may be willing to help at a discounted rate given the situation, or have a "sliding scale" fee structure to assist those with financial challenges.

Another option is to ask on social media if anyone knows a counselor that has experience dealing with grief and loss. It is important to select a profession who has had the opportunity to work with many families and people experiencing grief. Typically, females like to work with females and males like to work with male therapists. If it is a couple attending counseling, a male or female can be appropriate.

If word of mouth or social media is not helpful, start researching Licensed Mental Health Counselors (LMHC) in your area. You can reach out via email or call to see if they are accepting new patients. If they are accepting new patients, it's important to share with them what your group is trying to do and who you are in relation to the person you are trying to help. From there, you will want to discuss cost and availability. Questions to ask:

- Do you have nights/weekends available?
- What is your typical cost per session?
- Is there any flexibility in your price per session?
- Is there paperwork you can send ahead of time?
- Is there a credit card authorization form I need to complete since payment will not be covered by the client?

Alternative: Often churches provide support with a resource of lay people who are trained through a nonprofit organization, Stephens Ministries. These are people who have a heart for the hurting and who do not charge anything. Also, some colleges, seminaries, and online universities have therapeutic counseling students in training that need hours. This may be an option in your area.

More Than "I'm Sorry"

(7)
SUPPORT

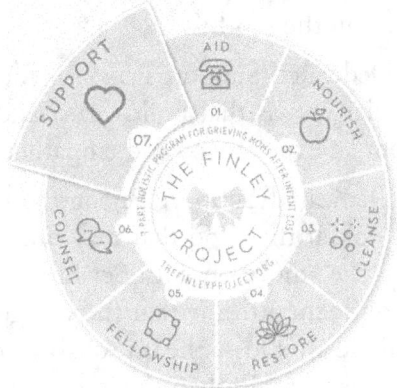

> "Start where you are. Use what you have. Do what you can."
>
> Arthur Ashe

A tip while helping with Support: The Head Coordinator doesn't have to be the only leader in the mission to help a grieving mom. Depending on the size of your helper group, you may need others to fill big and sometimes time-consuming roles. Everyone has the same goal of supporting the mother, but the way each person contributes and participates can be personal to them. That's okay. Be sensitive to how your volunteers are responding and accomplishing their tasks. Be flexible and help people find ways to be supportive that also work for them.

Example of Support:

Dedicated Support Person

Why is a Dedicated Support Person important? One person needs to be committed to providing consistent attention and compassion, two elements vital to healing from a tragic loss. This person is the primary listening ear and gives much-needed encouragement and a shoulder to lean on. What can happen when there is no "Dedicated" Support Person is that everyone assumes that others are "being there" for the mother when they are not able to give her their attention. Or a mom may have others around, but not a person who can truly relate to what she is going through. This usually results in wide gaps in support, which can be very hard on the mother.

A Dedicated Support Person is ideally someone who has experienced a similar loss as that builds trust and rapport that the support is coming from an experienced and empathetic place.

A Dedicated Support Person's job is not to press the grieving mother to look at the good that may one day come from her loss, nor to insist that she "move on with her life." Their role is to simply have and share a confident attitude that she will get through this and that there is hope and life after loss. She is probably not a professional or someone with "all the answers." Rather, she is a heart-to-heart listener and helper who can hold firm and say, "I made it, you can too."

When someone loses a child, there are often well-meaning family and friends around. The faces are familiar, but the mother knows that unless personally experienced, no one truly understands what it feels like to lose their own small child.

This is why I say that it may be that the best Dedicated Support Person would be a woman who has walked through this same kind of grief before. Losing a child is not a typical loss, no matter what anyone imagines. The feelings associated with grief like intense sadness, hurt, anger, and despair are amplified to a level that is scary. It's a deep despair that is so unfamiliar that it is hard to see out of. When a grieving mother meets someone who has a similar experience, all of these feelings feel less scary because they share a commonality with someone else. They feel less ostracized and alone because their feelings are often validated and affirmed by another. This cohesive connection helps a grieving person take steps forward, knowing that they are not abnormal for feeling such intense pain and that they can make it with the help of someone else.

The Finley Project is blessed to have help from some amazing women who have gone through the tragedy of losing a child, including Jerilyn Hughes-Lorch. Jerilyn is a very special woman who has dedicated her life to helping others after losing her daughter Kristina in 1978. For 20+ years, Jerilyn has poured her heart into helping grief-stricken women all over the country by sharing her story. Jerilyn shared with us about serving as a Volunteer Support Coordinator: "I hope to prepare moms for the unexpected emotions, especially in the first year. Each mother walks their own unique path and I hope to help them in that journey while honoring their precious angel."

(7) SUPPORT

Jerilyn and daughter Kristina Michelle (1978)

One mother, Parecia DeGuzman explains, "After losing Elin, my Support person was the first person I talked to who actually understood what I felt. I had heard all the clichés from everyone else, but when we started talking, I felt peace! She seemed to read my mind, and express all that I was feeling, but trying to contain. She also convinced me to finally go to counseling, which ultimately saved my life."

How to find this person? Ask around for someone who has experienced a similar loss. Call your local church or synagogue and ask if they have a Grief Support group and contact its leader. You can even turn to social media to share a general request for someone who has experienced a specific type of loss that your friend/family is going through.

Importantly, please know that just because someone has been through this kind of loss does not mean they would be a good choice for supporting the mom you are helping. You and your group will need to check a person's stability and where they are in their own grief process. Just because a person lost a child years ago does not mean they are in a healthy space to support someone else. Do they go to counseling? Have they done the work that put them in a healthy place to help someone else? These are important things to find out when connecting them with a grieving mother. Remember, you are the buffer, so you have to protect the grieving person from more damage.

When asking a support person if they can help someone else, don't hesitate to ask them about their own story of loss and grief. And tell them about the mom you are wanting to help. You will want to paint the entire picture so that they can decide if they can handle the situation or not. Don't be afraid to ask, "Is this someone you would feel comfortable talking with and supporting?" Acknowledge that it is a heavy situation and it's okay if it feels "too hard."

One of the main issues The Finley Project program has encountered (and I have seen in support groups) is the problem of a support person (or group leader) turning the focus back on their own story. It is important when leading others to allow the space to be filled with the grieving person's pain, NOT the support person's pain. Over time, a support person can share their story, but it imperative that early on, the relationship is about the newly grieving person's story.

How can you and your "Core Group" continue to offer support for the months and years to follow?

I will never forget how Lane Alexander supported me in my darkest time. She had been a friend I knew since high school whom I later played collegiate volleyball with, becoming one of my closest friends and still is to this day. Lane was at the hospital when Finley took her last breath and was there for me at my home, bringing me meals and checking on me.

Lane did something extraordinary, something I still cherish every time I see it. Lane reached out to me EVERY single 25th day of each month since Finley died. It was something simple such as "Thinking of you today" and included a pink bow or a little girl emoji. This commitment to follow up has made me feel less alone and not forgotten. I am so thankful that Lane has never, ever forgotten my Finley.

Note the importance of both immediate/short-term support and ongoing long-term support. Never hesitate to reach out when the thought occurs, but you definitely want to pull together a supportive group to make sure there is consistency. For example, you could set a calendar reminder on your phone to remind you to make the phone call, send a "thinking of you" card, or even a simple, caring text message. Share this idea with others who want to be supportive throughout those first extremely challenging weeks and months.

> "I am so thankful that my dear friend Lane has never ever forgotten my Finley."
>
> Noelle Moore, a mom who's been there

(7) SUPPORT

Lane Alexander & Noelle Moore, Orlando, FL (2013)

Lane Alexander & Noelle Moore, Finley's Celebration of Life, Winter Park, FL (2014)

There are unlimited ways you can make a grieving person feel supported long term, like I was so blessed to experience. Here are some ideas:

- LONG TERM: The goal is to think "long term." Often people feel forgotten after a few weeks or months, when everyone goes back to work, their lives, their friends.
- CONSISTENT: It is important to follow up on a regular basis, even if the person doesn't respond or say too much.
- REACH-OUT: There are many ways to reach out so the grieving mom feels less alone and disconnected. Here are some ideas:
- Set a calendar reminder on your phone, a certain day each month to send a text. You can say something simple: "thinking of you today."
- Set a calendar reminder to send a card in the mail or an e-card every month for a year. The message can be simple: "You and your little angel are not forgotten." "You are Loved." "Your precious angel loves you."

Apply Each Step as Soon as Possible

My hope is that you and your friend group, co-workers, and family members now feel more equipped to help the hurting mom than you were before reading this book. Know that your efforts and love will not be in vain. Although loss is incredibly complicated, I believe these seven

More Than "I'm Sorry"

steps will help for the long haul. Are there a lot of other things that can be done? Yes. Can you add other things to help? Of course. But these seven things are a roadmap to help build a healing foundation for the mother and father for many years to come. Now go ahead and start planning who is going to help and your next steps. The hurting family needs you!

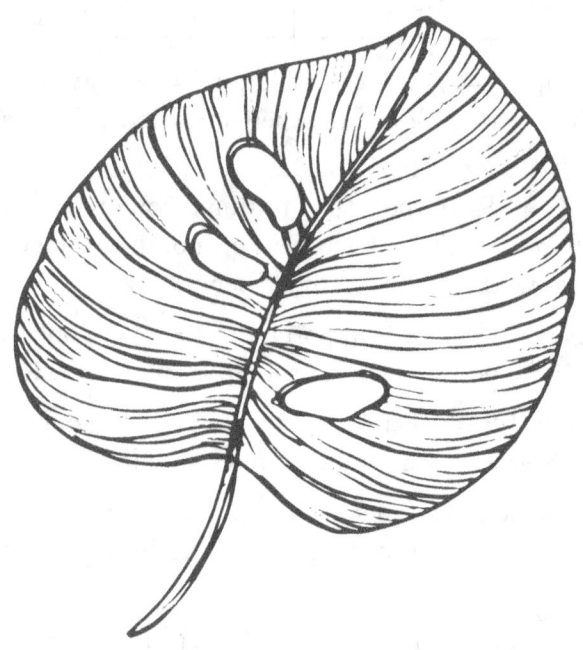

CHAPTER 10

Honor and Hope

> "Hope deferred makes the heart sick, but a longing fulfilled is a tree of life"
>
> Proverbs 13:12

I often refer to the "elephant in the room," which is people not knowing whether they should talk about the deceased child, or not. Their thoughts make them feel confused, suppressed, or like heading for the door. What are the worries?

- "I don't want to upset them."
- "I don't know what to say."
- "What if they get mad?"
- "It's weird to keep talking about it."
- "Maybe if we just don't talk about it, they will forget for just a bit."
- "They should be looking ahead, not at the painful past."

One thing is true for any and every grieving mother and father: they have not forgotten about their child, nor will they ever forget, all the rest of their lives. The child's face, their smile, their name —all are woven into the tapestry of everyday life.

As the wind blows, as the sun shines, a child is forever in a mother and fathers' essence. Mothers share with me that upon awakening from sleep, their first awareness is of the child, followed by the cruel truth that they are gone. "After I mentioned to my friend that today would have been my daughter's one-month birthday, he said he had realized that but 'didn't want to bring it up.' Wow. Like she wasn't already brought up and on my mind? Like if he didn't mention her, I would surely be not thinking about her at all, but something else?..."

So, generally, you should not avoid mentioning their child, while being sensitive to how ready they are to spend much time talking about their lost son or daughter. Usually, to talk about their child just brings to light what so many are thinking about and missing – their little one. Even if you never knew or saw the child, there are different ways to talk about him or her which make the mother or father feel supported and even a little comforted. You can include "observations" you could share, as well as "comments" that allow them to share. Here are a few examples of each:

Observations

- I saw a butterfly and thought of your daughter [or use name].
- This song reminded me of your son.
- Your daughter had your beautiful blue eyes.

Comments for Sharing

- Do you want to share what you miss about your daughter/son?
- How are you REALLY doing?
- What is one thing you think you really need to understand? Are struggling with the most?
- What is the hardest part about walking through this?

No matter how brief their life, most little ones who die have a given name and their name never dies, even when they do. To mention a child's name acknowledges that they lived and that their life has meaning. Say their name around the grieving person and if they aren't ready to talk, they will let you know.

Go ahead and make some observations or opening comments. Do not avoid this topic and talk instead of other people and things. This may not bother some grieving moms, but for others, you are dishonoring the life and memory of a person who will always be important to them. Show that you aren't opposed to talking about the child and be an open door for them. Do not be afraid to mention, ask, listen, and honor.

A Unique Journey of Grief that Requires Long-Term Support

It is not natural to outlive one's child. The pain heals over time, but the scars are permanently part of the mother's heart and spirit. To be supportive, think "long term." Not many people will, but you can.

The long-haul game is where people need others more than it is known. Throughout the long game, there are different things that can be done:

- Send a card every week for a year.
- Send a text once a week, letting the hurting person know you remember the loved one lost. Be sure to say the baby's name.
- Take the person to dinner, allow them to share.
- Invite them to events. It's okay if they say *no*, but keep inviting, again and again and again.
- Plan a trip.
- Put together an online fundraiser in their loved one's honor.
- Offer to visit the cemetery or special place with them.
- Plan a scrapbook night.
- Take a walk with her.
- Encourage the father or partner to attend counseling and support groups with the mom.
- Encourage the mom to give the father some space if he's not ready to go to counseling or a support group (men process differently).
- Some families have other living children. Encourage the mother and father to talk about the loss with them if the children are old enough to talk and share. Also suggest a local grief center or counselor who specializes in helping children process grief.

Bobbi shares: "Two examples of wonderful things people did to honor my daughter:

Many people sent me sympathy cards, called, or came over. There was an outpouring of concern and "so sorry" wishes, which were appreciated then and now. There was plenty of focus on me, but not that much on my poor innocent daughter, Mariel Elisabeth, who had lost her life. Here are two examples of the most thoughtful, going-the-extra-mile things that were done to honor my daughter who died way too young. These were not my idea nor at my request. It's now been over ten years ago, but I'm filled with gratitude just recalling these expressions of heart-felt support.

1. I wasn't really ready to drive, but I was driving myself somewhere when my phone rang. I could answer it hands-free and did so. It was Sam, a client of mine, who had already sent me a sympathy card but wanted to do something more…yes, more than "I'm Sorry." When I realized what he was asking, that he wanted me to help him find the perfect way to memorialize my daughter, I had to pull off the side of the road as I started to sob. The eventual outcome is that he started a project through the Atlanta Humane Society, which would be an ongoing "humane heroes award" in my daughter's name to recognize children who had shown kindness to animals.

2. A friend since high school, Roger, asked a mutual friend, Michele, to paint one of her artistic signs. He lived in a different state than me, so I only saw what he did to honor my daughter through photos he sent me until years later, when I visited "Mariel's Garden" in person. He planted beautiful flowers, including peace lilies and amaryllis, and in front of the huge flower bed is the lovely "Mariel's Garden" sign. He has tended that garden and sent me pictures all these years.

This is all I want—to know that others join me in tending to and nurturing the memory of my daughter."

A Mom Needs Ways to Honor Her Child

As with Bobbi, many times a mom is grateful to learn that others have found ways to honor her child. There may have even been suggestions provided if there was an obituary or printed program at a Funeral or Celebration of Life event. Also, some mothers have a deep personal need to express a special way of memorializing their lost child, something they actually do themselves. For those, one way of honoring a child can be done through helping others. In 2014, approximately six months after Finley's death, I had a friend reach out to me and share that a good friend of hers had lost her son. She wanted to see if I was able to talk to her friend and offer support.

I was terrified. I wasn't sure what I would say or how I would say it, but I gently urged myself to "go back to how it all first felt" and "remember what people said to you that helped." So that is what I did. I allowed myself to go within, into a painful but beginning-to-heal place to then talk to this mother. I asked the hard questions, "What is the hardest part about all of this?" I listened. I asked, "How are you *really* doing?" I listened with every ounce of compassion I had.

She later said that I'd made a huge difference for her because I allowed her to share, I acknowledged her son, and she felt less alone. You can be that person helping someone who is in pain, giving them hope to keep going.

The word "hope" started to really run through my mind as the years moved through. I also began to wonder what "honor" looks like, not just for me, but for others. For me, *to honor* meant to live my life in a way that makes meaning out of Finley's death. For others, honor looks much different. For me, there was no honor without hope. I had to have my own purpose in this life in order to create meaning.

One Friday morning in 2021, I walked into my sun-filled patio, happy to know that the weeks' end was finally here, and a weekend filled with hours for sleeping and some fun activities were about to begin. As I stepped onto my porch, about to sit down for my morning ritual of reading the Bible and journaling all things good and bad, I pictured in my mind H-O-P-E. An image formed of an acrostic for HOPE. The black letters appeared in my mind:

H – Having
O – Our (OWN)
P – Purpose
E – Everyday

HOPE: The Finley Project Moms, Orlando, FL (2017)

According to Dr. William Worden, who developed the ideology of the "Tasks of Grieving," one must "find connections with the deceased in the midst of embarking on a new life" as a part of grieving and healing.

For me, I had to have HOPE, a purpose in my life's existence, in order to figure out how to honor my daughter's life. I had to find a connection with Finley's life and death, in order to keep going. Without hope, or purpose, getting out of bed felt impossible. Without purpose, living doesn't even feel like an option. I have been there. I have felt the pain of not knowing why my body still stands on this earth.

These words rang loud in my head: "Hope deferred makes the heart sick, but a longing fulfilled is a tree of life." – Proverbs 13:12.

Without hope, the body doesn't feel like going on or moving through days, but when vision, purpose and a "why" is defined, a person has a reason to keep living.

For some, it's finding hope in going back to school, finding new courage, trying a new endeavor like music or art, or making extended travel plans—maybe to see family or friends for a long overdue visit (death is always a reminder than every life has an expiration date and putting off seeing someone can mean you lose that opportunity). For others, the sense of purpose gets channeled into their other children or working on strengthening their marriage.

Honor and Hope

There are countless ways a mother or father can honor their little one. Honor takes many forms. Finding one's purpose after loss will pave the way for honor to happen. Sometimes people just want to be a kinder human or an advocate for change. Some choose to process privately and share only with close friends and family; others want to start an organization. Some want to build a world-changing nonprofit organization named for the precious child they lost!

My path to purpose is unique and I often share that I do not recommend starting a nonprofit organization. Kind of ironic, right? Considering I now manage the nation's only 7-Part Holistic Program for mothers after infant loss? It takes hours upon hours to get things rolling, thicker skin upon thicker skin as people often don't get it—and many more tears come than smiles for the first, long while.

For the Hanson family, the decision was made to honor their daughter, 6-day old baby Avery, who died in 2012 of sudden infant death syndrome. The Hanson family set up a family foundation called "Avery's Light," where they held fundraising events to then give back to various initiatives. One year, they chose a local elementary school to be the benefactor of their Annual Golf Tournament — it was the school Avery would have attended. The next few years, they chose different organizations and initiatives, eventually selecting The Finley Project to be their Golf Tournament benefactor. The Hansons honor their daughter through giving back and serving other families.

Eddy & Crystal Hanson with supporters of Avery's Light (2019)

More Than "I'm Sorry"

CHAPTER 11

My Mission to Improve Mother's Care in Hospitals

Advocating for change is a way to honor a little one gone too soon. One of the ways I did this was to dip my head into the mess of hospital staffing and why my Finley died. I could not fathom what I began to learn and could not shake it. I had to do something. I couldn't wrap my head around the notion that an OBGYN was not present at the hospital when I needed help!

A crazy thought, right? To think that there isn't an OBGYN at a hospital, full time, when a woman needs care, is crazy isn't?

I was shocked to learn that there was not full time OB coverage at all hospitals around the country. I realized that something must be done to help prevent more deaths and injuries of babies and mothers. I started talking. I started telling my family, friends and neighbors that they must understand a hospital's staffing structure before choosing a hospital. They must inquire as to who is on property and if the person always stays on property.

After sharing my story and trying to convince women not to use hospitals that don't have 24-hour coverage, I started seeing some friends and others make different choices. Women wanted to make sure they were constantly cared for, so they chose other hospitals that provided such 24-Hour OB Care. Jill Francoforte is one of these women.

An acquaintance turned friend, Jill ultimately made a choice that saved her life and her son's life. After a placenta abruption that could have killed both her and her son, Jill survived to tell her story.

> "Our friend (Noelle) who experienced the unimaginable is the next person who I believe saved our lives. She went through a horrible tragedy 4 months after our daughter was born in 2013. Her daughter did not make it. We shared the same OB with our daughters' pregnancies and delivered at the same hospital. Through her story and what she experienced at the other hospital, we decided that I could never have another baby there. We were certain that we wanted to have another baby sooner than later, so we had to make a decision as to where we wanted to get prenatal care.
>
> A good friend of mine highly recommended a different OB/GYN proactive. I made a consultation visit with her 5 months after Kennedy was born to get established at their office. She suggested that I wait until our daughter was 1 until we try and get pregnant with our second baby so that my body can fully recover from the surgery. So, we listened. I found out I was pregnant again 1 week before her 1st birthday! I felt like I made the right decision the entire time I was pregnant and would visit their office. I felt so comfortable knowing that I would be delivering at the new hospital and that I would be at one of the best hospitals in the world.
>
> I can't tell you that I would have made all of these decisions if it weren't for my friend. I learned from her story that the other hospital that we delivered at didn't have a Level 3 NICU. Depending on the situation with the baby, they would have to get transferred to another hospital to receive the level of care that is needed. In her case that happened, and it was too late. I learned that sometimes you have minutes or maybe seconds for the baby and mom to survive. I learned that you need to be at a hospital who can handle everything at that specific hospital. I also learned that they didn't have an OB laborist at the hospital 24/7. You had to wait until your OB showed up to the hospital. I learned a lot. I learned to trust my gut and I knew that I needed to be at the new hospital for this second pregnancy. Words cannot express how I feel towards our friend. I believe that her daughter is looking down on us and she

is Mason's angel. Had I not made any of these decisions to change OB's to ensure we would deliver at the new hospital; I truly do believe that Mason and I would not be here."

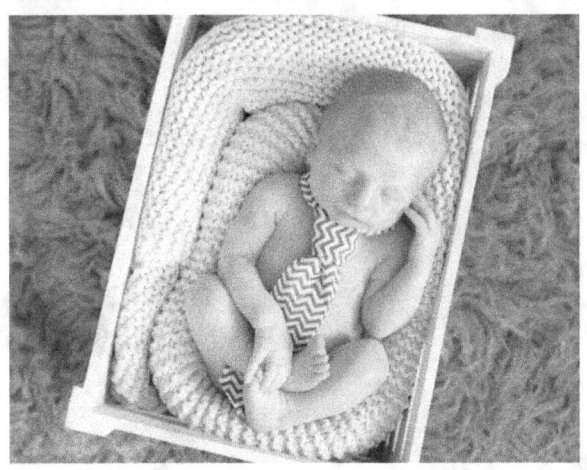

Mason Francoforte, Orlando, FL (2013)

On the flipside, another friend, Casey Knight chose to stay at her delivering hospital, but it was there that an OB Hospitalist, a doctor on staff and on property, saved her and her daughter's life.

> "At 29 weeks pregnant, I was sent to the hospital after discovering I had extremely high blood pressure. I was admitted and put on medications to lower my blood pressure. After a couple hours of monitoring and medicine, I felt a gush, and was terrified to find bright blood on the pad. We called in our nurse who did an exam and found the blood was coming from my cervix. She quickly called the doctor on call for my OB (my OB was out of town) and the high-risk obstetrician hospitalist. The hospitalist appeared in my room almost immediately, checked me out, and told the nurse to get me prepped for a C-section, and told my husband and I that it was going to be okay, but that my placenta was abruption and they had to get the baby out immediately. The nurse told her that she thought they should wait until my on-call OB got there and made the call. The hospitalist calmly, but firmly, said, "No, we need to get the baby out now. The on-call OB made it in time for the C-section, along with the hospitalist, and an additional OB due to the high risk of the situation, and they delivered my sweet 2 lb 7 oz baby girl.

We thank God that we were already at the hospital when my placenta abrupted and that the hospitalist made the quick call for the C-section. If they would have waited, it is likely that both the baby and I would have not survived. We're so thankful our hospital had an on-staff high risk hospitalist who was able to make the call and save mine and my baby's life!"

Casey Knight, Oklahoma, OK (2016)

I cannot profess to be a Physician, Hospital Administrator or even a skilled subject matter expert on OB staffing, yet I believe my plot in life is to use my tragedy to help develop as many OB Hospitalist Programs in the country so that women are safer. I also believe my role in sharing my story is so that OB Hospitalists and Private Practice Physicians know more about the importance of working together. The purpose is for the greater good and the safety of mothers all over the globe.

Things are changing and along with that is a notion that medicine is moving faster and requirements are more stringent. People's expectations are higher while documentation, liabilities and pressures rise. In the years I have been watching from the inside and outside of OB Hospitalist programs, I have seen and been told about the dichotomy between those employed within the hospital four walls and those stepping in periodically, as their patients are admitted.

This wherein is where the problem lies. I have seen where a Private Practice Physician didn't want a Labor & Delivery (L&D) nurse to call the OB Hospitalist on the floor because the Private Practice Physician wanted to be the one to do the emergency c-section. In turn, the nurse was put in a predicament where she had to decide where her loyalty stood – with the Patient, the OB Hospitalist or the Primary Private Practice Physicians. From my perspective, the reason these two groups do not get along and work as they should is pride and ego.

I know physicians get into medicine to help and to serve others, hopefully as some part to their motivation, but the inability to place the patient at the forefront of decisions is creating problems. Not all or even most Private Practice OBs are thinking this way, but for those who will not drop their ego to accept help, are creating the chasm.

Yes, there are fee structures and possible incentives for the OB Hospitalist to perform the act of delivery, but is waiting on the arrival of a Private Proactive OBGYN worth the wait? Is it worth a baby being injured? Is it worth a baby dying because of ego or comfortability?

Therefore, it is imperative that Hospitals work hard at creative a symbiotic team and cohesion amongst on property OB Hospitalists and incoming Private Practice Physicians.

Most women want their own OBGYN to deliver their child. I get it. However, I choose to honor my daughter by strongly urging women all over the world to be unashamed of understanding hospital staffing and to trust that an OB Hospitalist will do the very best they can to assist if the mother needs help. Would a mother rather run the risk of their baby suffering severe brain damage or death because they wanted to wait for someone they knew? Or would they trust the OB Hospitalist who is on property and able to help within seconds if needed?

OB Hospitalist have a noble calling and one that takes a special and patient person. I see OB Hospitalist as having the ability to step in, when necessary, step back when needed and to take charge as situations arise. OB Hospitalist should be valued as many set aside their private practice to step into a role that is still being defined at many hospitals, yet their willingness to want to help, is what makes them noble.

Armed with my newly acquired knowledge of hospital staffing, and my passion for OB Hospitalist programs, I demanded that the hospital where Finley died make changes. I committed to helping them from the beginning and not harming them. I met with their legal team, their Chief Medical Officer, Chief Operating Officer, their Medical Director, and a plethora of others multiple times over a two-year span, to insist they figure out how to develop an OB Hospitalist program. After years of asking and prodding, I am proud to share that this hospital system finally developed an OB Hospitalist Program where 20+OBGYN and Midwives were initially hired to serve in the role of providing 24-hour care.

I am proud to share that I honored Finley by starting "Know Moore Consulting."

Know Moore Consulting helps in two ways:

1. Educates others to *know more* about hospital staffing;
2. Educates, empowers, and coaches others how to help after child loss and how to help others turn over a new leaf to face a new season.

I will continue to work tirelessly to make life after loss easier for mothers and I urge you, dear readers, to join that cause. Also, I find myself more and more living with purpose, committed to making an impact around hospital staffing, OB care, and The Finley Project.

AFTERWORD

Reflections on Family, Faith, and the Future

"Come on, Dad! Let's go!" I yelled as I ran down the driveway. My dad was just finishing drying the hood of his shiny yellow over-sized sedan. It was a 1987 Cadillac Fleetwood.

Dad answered, "Okay, all set!" and placed the stained drying cloth on its shelf in the garage, then grabbed our faded orange basketball from the bucket. It was Sunday afternoon and the courts were waiting for us.

I was seven years old and this was our thing. The truth is that I just loved doing anything with my dad, but our mutual love of basketball defined our time together whenever we could manage it. We walked down to the end of the street, laughing and talking. We then proceeded to enter the gate to the neighborhood park, our own little world away from the world. It was there that my dad and I got to spend time together, drill after drill, shot after shot.

Red-faced, sweaty…no matter, I never gave up. I wanted to impress my dad. He truly did seem impressed.

It was spending time with both my dad and mom that made me feel loved and secure. They both made me feel loved and cherished.

I saw my mother as an amazing woman, mother, teacher, and encourager. My dad I saw as a successful businessman, father, former Marine and friend to many. I knew that when I grew up, I wanted to be like both my dad and my mom.

The years zipped by as grades passed, events were attended, games were played, family gatherings were had. Our family saw its share of marriages…and divorces that followed. My eyes saw hard times as the years moved forward, but there was this underlying foundation there, thanks to my parents—resiliency and survivorship.

You see, my mom had a very hard life, my dad did also, but neither one of them ever quit. My parents trusted in God and had the mentality that one must pull themselves up by their bootstraps and press on. Not finishing something was rarely an option in my house (except for one soccer league I quit). Discipline, structure, order, and completion were all staples in our home. It could sound like a tough style of my Marine dad, but actually the atmosphere could not have been more loving and my parents always made me feel special.

My dream of being a wife, mom, and working woman were planted inside of my heart and mind from a young age. I always wanted that, but God had a different path for me. My earlier "sunny" life was followed by hard times, pain, despair, confusion, and grief, but the resiliency I saw throughout my life is what allowed me to survive the unimaginable—the loss of my daughter.

Now years after the death of my sweet Finley, the loss of my father, and my husband leaving me, I have found peace. My faith in God was instilled deep in my heart since I was a child. I had always heard of and known of God's love, but I never had to rely solely on it until I lost everything. I was stripped of everything, only to make me look up.

Noelle Moore

I have found a strength that can only be attributed to God's power because without something supernatural, I would not have made it through the darkest of times.

Afterword

I've learned that whether I'm aware or not, God is always there. I remember the night my husband left. I was lying in my bed in deep despair. No text from a friend, no book I could pick up, no bringing my loving family to mind gave me any comfort at all. My last grasp at hope had me cry out to God, saying, "It's just you and me. You are all I have!"

I believe that character and reliance on God is developed when we experience tragedy and loss. I have felt the peace that only He gives. I had all the things I was taught about God sitting right in front of me and yet I was left to wrestle. *Was God real? Is there a heaven? Where did we come from? Is all that was taught to me true?* Like the Psalmist David, I grappled with understanding, but eventually came back to accept the Word of God.

I distinctly remember having a conversation with God after a BAD night. I had come home to an empty house and literally sunk down onto the kitchen floor. I sobbed and yelled so much, the back of my throat hurt. My eyes couldn't see, and I told God, "I am done! I am no longer a Christian. I don't believe You love me, or You are real, or You are here!" I was mad.

I know that some people reading this book shudder at this denouncing of my faith, but guess what? It's true and it's real and it happens. I have seen it in my own life and other hurting peoples' lives. What eventually happened is my hardened spirit was pursued by the Lord. Like a child after a temper tantrum, the post tantrum exhaustion had set in, and I just couldn't do it anymore.

But before this, I spent weeks and months with nowhere to turn. But I just kept running, filling my time with shopping, traveling, binge-eating, and eventually working out again. I didn't want to deal with my relationship with God, the universe, or eternity. However, eventually I was exhausted. I couldn't outrun the only love that never left me, never judged me, never got mad at me. I finally stopped and surrendered it all to the Lord.

I surrendered my anger, my hatred for the doctors, my husband and his family. I surrendered to the process of being shaped, molded, refined to be used by Him. What was my greatest inspiration for this change of heart? My angel, Finley Elizabeth. I told God one day, "If I am going to believe in heaven and seeing Finley again one day, then I have to believe in ALL you say in your Word and all of who you are." That changed it all for me.

I started to make meaning out of my pain and recognized that maybe, just maybe, God knew I could have this experience empower me to help others, even though I was hurting.

It was Christmas, 2014, and The Finley Project had just started. I was in church and was thinking about Mary, Jesus' mother. *What did it feel like for her to lose her only son? What emotions did she have, watching her son suffer and die on the cross?* Then I heard the voice of the Lord: "Finley died so others could live."

That's a big pill to swallow. I was overwhelmed with anger, humility, pain, love, confusion. How could this be her story? How could this be my story? I thought of mothers who were saved because they chose to not go the hospital where I delivered, for fear of there not being an OB on property, like Jill Francoforte.

I thought of the babies who were safely delivered by an OB Hospitalist because there was an OB on property at the time that they needed help. I thought of the sweet mothers that were starting to come into The Finley Project program and all those who would eventually come into the program, and how the hope we bring them could save their life.

I have been to hell and back and survived. *Seen Hell, got the t-shirt.* But really, I cannot write this book without sharing that hope can be found in any situation and that oftentimes, we go through something awful and hard, to then be the catalyst for change.

Now, because of Finley and me, many babies and mothers will be saved as a result of full-time staffing at this area hospital.

If my husband hadn't made the choice to leave me, then I never would have started The Finley Project. Everything does work together to make a unique story for each person, but will you choose to help make some else's story whole? Will you be the one who can bring a mom into a healing journey uniquely hers, but supported by you and her friends?

I was that mom that desperately needed help. I was that mom that wanted people to say "More than I'm Sorry." My hope is that my life and all that I have been through are all things you can lean into for inspiration and strength to help someone who is in need. You have the tools, the intention, the big heart…You've got this!

Afterword

Everett Alexander, Orlando, FL (July 2013)

The Finley Project Moms, Winter Park, FL (2021)

More Than "I'm Sorry"

Resources and Consulting

The Finley Project serves mothers in Central Florida and across the United States who have suffered stillbirth or the death of an infant from 22 weeks' gestation to 2 years of age. Our program supports mothers through the initial crisis following the loss and helps them to better manage their grief in order to reduce the long-term impact of this unique and tragic experience.

The Finley Project is the ONLY organization nationwide utilizing a holistic model to support bereaved mothers after infant loss. Our unique support program meets the practical as well as the emotional needs of mothers.

Healing is a process that takes time, so The Finley Project also continues to provide support to mothers for five years after they complete the initial program.

> "What a fantastic organization! It is literally responsible for saving lives."
>
> Dr. Anthony Orsini
> Neonatologist
> Founder and President of the "Orsini Way/Breaking Bad News"

> "Your mothers are a testament to all that you do. I get strength from watching your amazing project. I am so honored to be a part of your mission. You make a difference every day, all in honor of sweet Finley."
>
> Dr. Darlene Calhoun
> Neonatologist

"Noelle Moore was going through some of the worst pain imaginable in 2013: First, her father passed away while she was five months pregnant. Then a medical accident during the birth led to the death of her daughter, Finley, two weeks later. And two weeks after that, Moore's husband filed for divorce and never returned to their house.

During this period of intense grief, Moore realized that there were very few holistic resources aimed at helping mothers get through the most catastrophic stages of loss, and decided to start an organization of her own, which became The Finley Project." *People Magazine* (May 18, 2021).

Know Moore Consulting was founded by Noelle Moore to help others know more about how to help a grieving mother. Know Moore Consulting was founded in 2014 and provides Coaching, Consulting, and Training to individuals and groups on how to help after loss using a proven Model. To learn more, please visit: www.knowmooreconsulting.com

To sign up for Weekly Reminders and tips on how to help, please go to: www.knowmooreconsulting.com

Gift Ideas For Moms

If someone asks you what they can give to Mom…

These are ideas contributed by The Finley Program moms of gifts they received and appreciated:

45 Thoughtful Things to Give a Grieving Mom

Jewelry

1. Necklace with child's initials
2. Locket with child picture inside
3. Angel bracelet
4. Necklace that says "Mama" or "Mom"
5. Angel wing earrings
6. Ring "angel feather"

Blankets

7. Custom quilt with child clothes
8. Custom blanket printed with child picture
9. Soft blanket (perhaps monogrammed with child's initials)

Stuffed Animals

    10. Bear with heartbeat

    11. Bear with ashes

    12. Weighted bear

    13. Stuffed animal wearing piece of child's clothing

Books/Journals

    14. Journal

    15. Personalized pen to go with a journal

    16. Book of quotations or uplifting prayers

    17. Magazines (to browse, lots of lovely photos, nature, travel spots, etc. when the grieving person isn't up to reading/focusing)

    18. A gift card for books (Amazon, Barnes-N-Noble, etc)

    19. Donating to the New York Public Library, which will place a customized bookplate in a book in its collection as commemoration

Other

    20. "Headspace" app has a dedicated (mindfulness) program for dealing with grief (1 yr subscription)

    21. Certificate of life prints

    22. Ultrasound art

    23. Memorial lanterns/candles

    24. Garden dedication plaque

    25. Soft robe & slippers

    26. Bubble bath/bath bomb

    27. Hot tea

28. Wind chime

29. Art showing family together

30. Christmas ornament with child's name

31. "Heaven In Our Home" engraved hurricane glass candle holder

32. Name a star. You can sponsor a star and the family gets a certificate with the child's name indicated as the official name of the star

33. Shadow box for memories/keepsakes

34. Box for keepsakes

35. Small heart-shaped stone

36. Sign for flower bed "Emma's Garden" (using the child's name)

37. Rose bush or other plant

38. Plant-a-Tree program

39. Stepping stone engraved with child's name

40. Personalized angel coffee mug (Etsy online has personalized everything)

41. Engraved photo frame

42. Embroidered pillow

43. Personalized socks

44. Original poem dedicated to the child

45. Outdoor angel statue (some have a solar light)

Know Moore Consulting educates, empowers, and coaches others on how to help after child loss – how to help others turn over a new leaf to face a new season.

If you found this book helpful, please leave a review on Amazon. Thanks!

For additional support, order your helpful companion book *More Than "I'm Sorry" CARE GUIDE* from Amazon.com, Barnes & Noble or any online bookseller.

Hospital Administrators, Counseling Groups, Business Owners and Others…

We appreciate you!

Contact Noelle Moore to learn how Know Moore Consulting can help you and your team help families in the best way after loss.

Go to www.knowmooreconsulting.com

and fill out the brief form.

ORDER CARE GUIDES for your group at a SPECIAL DISCOUNT here:

www.knowmooreconsulting.com

www.ingramcontent.com/pod-product-compliance
Lightning Source LLC
Chambersburg PA
CBHW050320120526
44592CB00014B/1992